BEOW

CHRIS MCCULLY, born in Bradford, Yorkshire in 1958, worked as a full-time academic, specialising in the history of the English language and on English sound-structure as well as on verse and verse-form, at the University of Manchester (1985–2003). From 2003–13 he worked part-time at various universities in the Netherlands (Vrije Universiteit, Amsterdam; Rijksuniversiteit Groningen) while writing books for several publishers. His *Selected Poems* (Carcanet) was published in 2012. He is currently a Senior Lecturer in the Department of Literature, Film and Theatre Studies at the University of Essex.

CHRIS McCULLY

BEOWULF

A translation and
a reading

Carcanet Classics

MMXVIII

First published in Great Britain in 2018 by
Carcanet
Alliance House, 30 Cross Street
Manchester M2 7AQ
www.carcanet.co.uk

A CIP catalogue record for this book is
available from the British Library,
ISBN 978 1 78410622 5

Typeset by Andrew Latimer in Sabon
Printed in Great Britain by SRP Ltd., Exeter, Devon

The publisher acknowledges financial
assistance from Arts Council England.

for
MONIKA
and in memory of
IAN MUNDY MCCULLY
(1915–61)

CONTENTS

ACKNOWLEDGEMENTS

It's proper to acknowledge the debt I owe to Steve Glosecki, who died far too young. The world of scholarship, of collegiate generosity, is smaller for his passing.

The following scholars have had, in different ways, at different times and in different places, a great and invariably kind influence on the present translation and the making of its apparatus: Sanja Bahun and audience members at the Essex Book Festival (2016), Martin Duffell (who in 2017 read the draft in its entirety with both Wrenn and Heaney alongside him), Simon Everett, John Gillies, Patricia Gillies, Kristin Hanson, Martin Harrison, Grevel Lindop, the Research Seminar in the Department of Literature, Film and Theatre Studies (University of Essex), Adrian May, Donka Minkova, Renos Papadopoulos, Ad Putter, Jordan Savage, Sean Seeger (who put me again in the way of Jameson's reading of pastiche), Jeremy Solnick (another full-draft reader, of precision and suggestiveness), Phil Terry and Tony Wood. My classes, too – particularly second-year writing students at the University of Essex – were sometimes exposed to bits of the translation and often had hugely interesting things to say. An audience at Chelmsford Public Library helped me to think about fabulous beasts during a workshop on Essex dragons (Essex Book Festival, 2017). The research seminar on Contemporary Poetry in Translation (University of Essex, 2017) also helped me onwards rejoicing – or if not quite rejoicing, then somewhat reassured. Of course none of these souls are responsible in any way for the errors I have made in the present work. Those errors, and the choices that underlay them, are mine.

Of older faces and voices, former colleagues at the University of Manchester should be acknowledged, chief among them my friend and erstwhile supervisor, Richard Hogg. Richard used to joke that I could quote at least the first third of Beowulf by heart, and although he was quite wrong about that, his kindness, patience and skill somehow brought me through a philological encounter with the poem in the later 1980s. And before Richard's editorial pencil ever got to work on the words of a hugely unpromising PhD student, my teachers at the University of Newcastle-upon-Tyne first taught me about this uncompromising, difficult Germanic world. I hope they will forgive what I have done here, and in particular, forgive my wrong-headedness and false start(s). I sometimes smile ruefully when I remember that his teachers found even Beowulf 'a No-good. On the mead-benches Geat commanders gave him no honour. He was of no account. He was slow, they said – slow or lazy. ("Too feeble," said the chiefs.)...'. And yet, adds the poet, 'a change happened [...]'. There is probably hope, at least, for most of us – until the dragon wakes again.

GENEALOGIES

Danes – also called *Spear-Danes, Ring-Danes, Bright-Danes, East- and West-Danes, Scyldings*

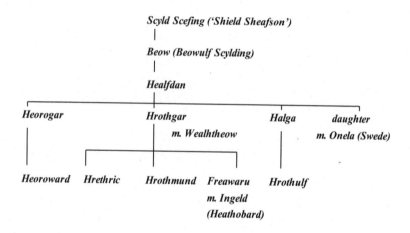

Scyld Scefing ('Shield Sheafson')
|
Beow (Beowulf Scylding)
|
Healfdan

Heorogar   Hrothgar   Halga   daughter
          m. Wealhtheow   m. Onela (Swede)

Heoroward Hrethric Hrothmund Freawaru Hrothulf
                        m. Ingeld
                      (Heathobard)

Genealogies

Geats– also called *Weder-Geats* ('Weather-Geats'), *War-Geats, Sea-Geats, Weders* and *Hrethlings*

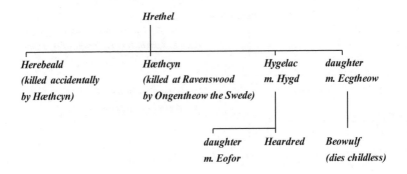

Swedes – also called *Scylfings* and *War-Scylfings*

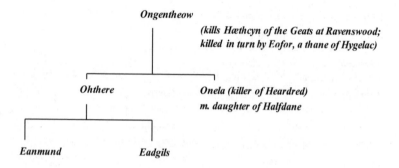

Ongentheow

(kills Hæthcyn of the Geats at Ravenswood; killed in turn by Eofor, a thane of Hygelac)

Ohthere

Onela (killer of Heardred)
m. daughter of Halfdane

Eanmund

Eadgils

PROPER NAMES

LINE REFERENCES: refer to the line in which the name is introduced into this translation.

NOTE ON SPELLINGS AND PRONUNCIATION: there is no silent letter-shape <e>, so that all syllables of e.g. *Aelfhere* (very roughly 'ALF+hay+ruh' where upper case = stressed) are pronounced. Combinations of letter shapes <sc> are pronounced 'sh', thus <Scyld>, 'Shield', <Scylfing>, 'SHIL+fing' and <Aeschere>, 'ASH+hay+ruh'. <h> is never silent, thus is pronounced in e.g. *Hnaef* and *Hrothgar*. The letter shape <g> is pronounced 'y' when it precedes high/mid-high front vowels, thus <Geat>, 'Yay+at'. All proper names bear stress on their initial (or in the case of monosyllables, their only) syllable. I have elsewhere, as throughout, transliterated the letter shapes thorn and eth found in the original to <th>.

It's useful to remember that royal succession was not necessarily based on primogeniture (the succession of the firstborn). While the firstborn child of a ruler would have a good claim to succeed to the throne, other family members – brothers, uncles – might be judged by the governing council of the tribe (the *witan*) to make more effective leaders. This *realpolitik* helps to account for the internecine feuding so commonly found in early Germanic literature; brothers fight against brothers, uncles against cousins.

Abel	108	Biblical figure, killed by his brother Cain.
Aelfhere	2604	A kinsman of Wiglaf; both belonged to the tribe of Scylfings.
Aeschere	1323	An old comrade of Hrothgar, killed by Grendel's mother. Aeschere was the older brother of Yrmenlaf.
Beanstan	524	Father of Breca, who (Unferth alleged) bested Beowulf in a swimming contest.
Beo(w)	18	Son of Scyld and grandfather of Hrothgar; part of the Danish royal line and not the protagonist of the poem.
Beowulf	343	The protagonist of the poem. His father was Ecgtheow, his mother unnamed – but his mother was a sister of Hygelac, king of the Geats, and therefore Hygelac was Beowulf's uncle.
Breca	506	Son of Beanstan and a prince of the Brondings. Undertook a swimming contest with the young Beowulf.
Brondings	521	Tribe governed by Breca.
Brosings	1199	Tribe who possessed the necklace ('bright-jewelled torc' in this translation) stolen by Hama when he was fleeing Eormanric of the Ostrogoths. In Norse legend, the necklace was first made for the goddess Freya (Wrenn/Bolton, p.293).
Cain	106	Brother and slayer of Abel. The poet claims that Cain is the ultimate ancestor of all things misbegotten and evil. (It's also worth noticing that just as the good and the great are presented in terms of tribe and genealogy, so evil too has an ancestry.)
Daeghrefn	2502	A Frankish warrior killed by Beowulf (with his bare hands) during Hygelac's wars against the Franks.

Danes   2   Also called *Spear-Danes, Ring-Danes, Bright-Danes, East-* and *West-Danes* as well as *Scyldings* (the last, the name of their pre-eminent ruling family in the context of the poem). Twice the poet also refers to Hrothgar's tribe as the *Ingwine* (1045, where I have translated Hrothgar into an 'Ingwin-Friend' and 1319, where I have translated him as 'Ingwin Hearth-Lord').

Eadgils   2392   A Swedish prince, son of Ohthere, whose brother Onela exiled him for rebellion. Eadgils went into exile in Geatland, where he lived under the protection of Heardred, the successor to Hygelac. Onela invaded Geatland and Hearded was slain, but Beowulf gained the Geatish throne and subsequently helped Eadgils take revenge on Onela.

Eanmund   2611   Brother of Eadgils. Killed by Weohstan (also rendered as Wihstan), the father of Wiglaf, a Waegmunding – a tribe within the tribe of Swedes or Scylfings – who assists Beowulf in his fight against the dragon.

Earnaness   3032   Literally the headland (*ness*) of the eagles (*earn+a*) – a promontory near where Beowulf met his death.

Ecglaf   499   The Danish father of the troublemaker Unferth.

Ecgtheow   263   Father of Beowulf and a Waegmunding; married to the only daughter of the Geat king Hrethel. Hygelac (one of Hrethel's sons) was therefore Beowulf's uncle by marriage.

Ecgwela   1710   An ancient king of the Danes.

Eofor   2486   (Also *Eafor*). The Geatish killer of the Swedish king Ongentheow. He was rewarded

lavishly by Hygelac and given Hygelac's
daughter in marriage (2997).

Eomer   1960   Son of Offa the Angle (an ancestor of Offa of
Mercia) and kinsman of Hemming.

Eormenric   1200   Ancient king of the Eastern (Ostro-) Goths
who committed suicide c. 376 CE.

Eruli   5   I have translated textual *Eorl[e]*, line 6 of the
originating text editions, as 'Eruli' follow-
ing Wrenn/Bolton. The Eruli were 'a notably fierce and powerful Germanic tribe...
who had a settlement in Denmark' (Wrenn/
Bolton, p.294, see also their footnote on
p.96). It seems contextually apt to describe
Scyld Scefing as terrifying the Eruli if the
Eruli had a reputation as one of the more
warlike clans he subsequently pacified.

Finn   1068   King of the Frisians. Married into the Danish ruling house – to Hoc's daughter Hil-
deburh. An episode in the poem – related
by Hrothgar's scop – recounts how Finn
clashed with Hildeburh's brother Hnaef.
Hnaef was killed but his retainer Hengest
assumed leadership of the remaining Danes.
Finn's and Hengest's respective forces pass
an uneasy winter in a hall but the truce is
eventually broken, Finn is killed and Hildeburh is brought back to Denmark by
Hengest's people.

Finns   581   The 'Finns' homeland' of line 581 here is
probably to be identified as the land of
the Lapps who then inhabited Finnheden
in Småland (SW Sweden). It's unlikely that
Beowulf could have been borne to north-
ern Norway (present-day Lapland) after

his swimming contest with Breca: it's more possible that the tides washed him ashore in southern Sweden.

Fitela	879	Nephew of the legendary king, the dragon-slayer Sigmund. (Sigmund's son Sigurd features as the renowned dragon-slayer of the *Edda* and is the Siegfried of the *Niebelungenlied*.)
Folcwalda	1089	The father of Finn.
Franks	1210	A tribe who occupied what is today part of the Netherlands. Hygelac lost his life in one of his campaigns against the Franks.
Freawaru	2023	Daughter of Hrothgar, promised in marriage to Ingeld the son of Froda, a Heathobard.
Friesland	1126	Territory of the tribe of Frisians, roughly corresponding to present-day Friesland, lying east and north of the Ijsselmeer.
Frisians	1070	Tribe occupying Friesland. East Frisians-fought with Finn against Hnaef; West Frisians fought alongside the Franks against Hygelac (Morgan, p.86; Wrenn/Bolton. p.295).
Froda	2025	King of the Heathobards and father of Ingeld.
Garmund	1962	Father of Offa, king of the Continental Angles.
Geats	206	Also called *Weder-Geats* ('Weather-Geats'), *War-Geats*, *Sea-Geats*, *Weders* and *Hrethlings*.
Goths	2494	The poet refers to Hygelac having no need to hire mercenaries from among the 'Gifthas' (in the manuscript – an East Germanic tribe). Wrenn/Bolton note that this tribe is the Gepidae, an East Germanic tribe who settled around the Vistula, north of present-day Slovakia. So obscure is this tribe, and

so relatively unimportant to the structure of the poem, that I have lumped together the Gepidae with the better-known Goths: 'For [Hygelac] there was no need / to get fighters from the Goths or Danes, / to seek and pay Swedish hire-swords'.

Grendel 102 Humanoid and rapacious monster.

Guthlaf 1148 A warrior fighting in Hnaef's – later Hengest's – Danish forces against Finn.

Haereth 1929 The father of Hygd, Hygelac's wife.

Haethcyn 2434 The Geat king Hrethel's second son, whose brothers were Herebeald and Hygelac. In a memorable passage, the poet tells how Haethcyn accidentally killed his elder brother Herebeald and how Hrethel is unconsolable (2463ff.). After Hrethel's death, Haethcyn succeeded to the Geatish throne but was subsequently killed by the Swedish king Ongentheow.

Half-Dane 1068 Wrenn/Bolton claim that 'Half-Dane' is a 'strange name' and conjecture that the Half-Danes in the poem (found in the 'Finn episode', 1067ff.) were a 'sub-tribe of Jutes in Danish service' (p.296).

Halga 61 Younger brother of Hrothgar.

Hama 1198 A warrior who carries off the Brosing necklace from Eormenric.

Healfdan 57 *Half-Dane* (proper name). Descendant of Scyld and Beow and father of Hrothgar. Spelled in the translation *Healfdan*, largely because I needed a word whose form was a heavy syllable (*Healf-*) followed by a lighter syllable *(-dan)*. The form *Healfdan* also helps to distinguish this personage from the tribe of Half-Danes – see *Half-Dane* above.

Heardred 2201 Son of Hygelac and Hygd for whom Beowulf acts as chief counsellor, having refused the Geatish throne in Heardred's favour. Heardred is killed in the subsequent war against the Swedes.

Heathobards 2302 Germanic tribe whose feud with the Danes is recounted in 2023ff., where Hrothgar's daughter Freawaru was promised in marriage to Ingeld, son of Froda of the Heathobards. That attempted tribal reconciliation would not end well (2032ff.).

Heatholaf 459 A Wulfing warrior killed by Ecgtheow, Beowulf's father.

Helmings 620 The tribe of Wealhtheow, wife of Hrothgar. Wrenn/Bolton identify the Helmings with the Wulfing tribe (p.296).

Hemming 1944 Kinsman of Offa and Eomer, of the Continental Angles.

Hengest 1083 Leader of the Half-Danes after the death of Hnaef.

Heorogar 60 Eldest son of Healfdan and brother of Hrothgar.

Heorot 79 The great Danish hall, 'Hart'.

Heoroward 2161 Eldest son of the Danish king Heorogar.

Herebeald 2434 Eldest son of the Geatish king Hrethel. Accidentally killed by his brother Haethcyn.

Heremod 901 A Danish king (apparently a forerunner of Scyld) and in the poem a dark, brooding and doomed figure explicitly contrasted with Beowulf.

Hereric 2206 Probably a royal Geat – Heardred's uncle (Wrenn/Bolton, p.297).

Hetware 2363 A Frankish tribe, allied with the West Frisians

		against whom Hygelac fought in his last expedition.
Hildeburh	1071	Finn's wife, originally belonging to the Scylding tribe. Returned to Denmark after Finn's death.
Hnaef	1068	Hildeburh's brother.
Hoc	1076	Father of Hildeburh and Hnaef.
Hondscio	2076	The first of Beowulf's Geatish companions to be devoured by Grendel.
Hreosnaburh	2477	A hill in Geatland around which the Swedes fought against the Geats after Hrethel's death.
Hrethel	374	King of the Geats, father of Herebeald, Haethcyn, Hygelac and a daughter he gave in marriage to Ecgtheow, Beowulf's father. Dies of grief.
Hrethric	1189	Son of Hrothgar, brother of Hrothmund.
Hronesness	2805	'Whale's+headland'. A promontory in Geatland where Beowulf's burial-mound was constructed.
Hrothgar	61	King of the Danes, son of Healfdan and younger brother of Heorogar.
Hrothmund	1189	Son of Hrothgar, brother of Hrethric.
Hrothulf	1016	Hrothgar's nephew, son of Halga (Hrothgar's younger brother).
Hrunting	1457	Unferth's fabled sword, which he lent to Beowulf before Beowulf's encounter with Grendel's mother.
Hunlafing	1142	I've taken this to name a warrior – Hunlaf+ing, 'son of Hunlaf' – in Hengest's retinue.
Hygd	1926	Hygelac's wife, daughter of Haereth. She offered the Geatish throne to Beowulf in place of her own son Heardred, who was too young to rule effectively.

Hygelac	196	King of the Geats and uncle of Beowulf.
Ingeld	2064	Son of Froda and in the royal line of the Heathobards.
Ingwin	1045	A term for Hrothgar's Danes.
Modthryth	1931	Wife of Offa, of the Continental Angles, contrasted (here) with Hygd. The passage in which 'Modthryth' appears is very tricky to understand, let alone translate; I have chosen to contrast the respective behaviours of 'Modthryth' and Hygd and also have retained the accounts of the 'drinkers' who reclaim something of 'Modthryth's' later reputation.
Naegling	2680	Beowulf's sword, apparently (Wrenn/Bolton) taken from Daeghrefn of the Franks, which he used in the fight with the dragon. Naegling shattered in the combat.
Offa	1951	King of the Continental Angles.
Ohthere	2381	Son of Ongentheow, king of the Scylfings (Swedes).
Onela	62	Brother of Ohthere and married into the Danish royal house.
Ongentheow	1968	King of the Scylfings, who killed Haethcyn of the Geats at Ravenswood. Ongentheow was in turn slain by Eofor, one of Hygelac's men.
Oslaf	1148	Danish warrior who fought against Finn.
Ravenswood	2925	Place in Sweden where Ongentheow killed Haethcyn.
Raumar	519	Following Wrenn/Bolton I've translated 'Heatho-Raemas' of line 519 as 'the Raumar', the name of a Norwegian tribe onto whose shoreline Breca was cast up.
Scyld Scefing	4	Danish king, the founder of the Scylding royal line. His name is composed of the elements

'Shield' followed by 'Sheaf' and then a suffix (*-ing*) that denotes family or tribe – or possibly, as here, 'son of'. His name therefore comprises elements of both the martial and the fertile; Heaney translated aptly as 'Shield Sheafson'.

Scylding   54   Descendants of Scyld, therefore a general term for the Danes.

Scylfing   2203   A general term for the Swedes.

Sigmund   875   Son of Waels, uncle of Fitela, and a dragon-slayer of old (884).

Swedish   2384   I use 'Swedish' in line 2384 as a general adjective to mean 'tribes settled in east-central Sweden' rather than one particular tribe. This emphasises Ongentheow's mode of ensuring allegiance across a wide geographical area settled by different tribes.

Swerting   1202   Hygelac's grandfather (or perhaps uncle – textual *nefa* can mean either).

Unferth   499   Son of Ecglaf and one of Hrothgar's counsellors (and his spokesperson). His name literally means 'un+peace': in the context of the poem he is certainly and at best a sceptic about Beowulf and was probably also a fratricide, see lines 1167–8. Yet he was not without courage, was generous (he lent Beowulf his sword, Hrunting) and Beowulf eventually treated him with a certain courtesy, returning Hrunting to him with thanks (1809).

Waegmundings   2607   The tribe – a sub-tribe, as it were, of the Geats – to which Wiglaf and Beowulf belong.

Waels   897   Father of Sigmund.

Wayland   454   The great smith of Germanic poetry. The

		corselet Beowulf wore to the fight with Grendel was worked by Wayland.
Wealhtheow	612	Queen of Hrothgar.
Weders	225	A synonym for the Geats.
Wendels	348	A tribe – probably the Vandals – to which Wulfgar, one of Hrothgar's chief retainers, belonged.
Weohstan	2602	Father of Wiglaf and slayer of Eanmund.
Wiglaf	2602	A warrior and kinsman of Beowulf, and the last of the Waegmunding tribe.
Withergild	2051	A Heathobard warrior.
Wonred	2971	A Geat, father of the warriors Eofor and Wulf.
Wulf	2965	Son of Wonred who was wounded by Ongentheow in the Geat-Swedish wars and was subsequently killed by Wulf's brother, Eofor.
Wulfgar	348	Significant warrior of the Wendel tribe.
Wulfings	461	A tribe to which Heatholaf (killed by Ecgtheow, Beowulf's father) belonged.
Yrmenlaf	1324	A Dane, younger brother of Aeschere, one of Hrothgar's longest-serving retainers and counsellors.

BEOWULF

Hear from yesterday,   from the yore-days,
of the Spear-Danes –   how sped by courage,
how doomed in blood   their best of men.
   It was Scyld Scefing,   their sure founder,
the Eruli's terror,   who overturned benches,   5
was rampant in the halls   of surrounding clans.
First a foundling,   far from his beginnings,
honour helped him flourish;   he was himself honoured
under the teeming heavens.   Even tribes distant
across dark whale-roads   owed duties to him.   10
He was good, that king –   and good was his heir,
yare in winters,   yielded by God-grace
as gift, comfort.   God saw their unease,
that of old they'd lived   too long lordless,
so the Life-Shaper,   the Light of Honour,   15
sent them comfort,   success in this world:
far-flung or near   in the northlands, Beow,
Scyld's after-comer,   shone by reputation.
Always it's fitting   that a fine young man
secure loyalty   for his later years   20
by lavish gift-giving   while he lives at home,
still under his father's   first sheltering,
so that whatever maulings come,   his men will be bound
in memory of promise: all parties thrive
by unforced gold-gifts,   free-handed givers.   25
   Scyld passed away   in his powers, travelled
at last into the Lord's   release and care.
They bore him at the end   to brink of the tide,

his chosen men,   as their chief had asked
when he wielded words   like weapons; carried him   30
and his reputation   to the tide's slow brim.
At the hythe the prow,   hung with winter,
was ready, ring-carved: right ship for chiefs.
And there they laid   their last, first leader,
their ring-giver,   in the roomy hold.   35
He lay in state.   Stripped from outlying
tribes, there were trinkets –   turned, ornamented:
fine-wrought war-things,   friends for his journey.
I've never heard of keel   more keenly or better
charged with war-gear,   chainmail, battle-bills.   40
This massed plunder   was piled into the ship
and lay on his breast: treasures   for the tide-reaches.
They did no less   in their due offerings
than was once done in   those winters past,
when he was cast – a child –   into the clutch of waves   45
alone, girt round   with a people's gifts.
Then they raised aloft   a royal standard –
it flew high over his head –   and let the sea have him,
gave him to the tide-sway   sadly, grieving
and mourning their loss.   Men cannot tell   50
with truth, whether they're king   or clansman, what shore
or foreland received   that royal freight.
     Then Beow became lord   of the best-known tribe
of Scyldings, was in turn   shaped to prosper,
for wealth, and flourished   after his famed parent   55
had left this life.   He also left a son,
the beloved Healfdan,   who led Scyldings
for years in battle   and was beyond praising.
Four fine children   he fathered all told,
each of them a leader.   Eldest was Heorogar;   60
blessed Halga and   Hrothgar were his brothers.
And I heard also... of a daughter,

who was Onela's bride   and bed-fellow.
   Hrothgar prospered,   was given power in war,
his warriors' honour.   All his retainers   65
readily obeyed him;   their ranks comprised
a mighty force.   And in his mind he weighed
commanding the making   of a meeting-place,
triumphal mead-hall   made fair by men,
one mightier than any   had ever heard mentioned,   70
and in it, to all –   to old and young –
to grant, share, deal   what God ordained
beyond what was already   owned by right in common.
It was told widely   that the treasures of many
peoples of middle-earth   were on their merit ordered   75
to adorn that dwelling.   And in due season,
by dint of will,   they were done, and ready
stood the wondrous hall   that some wordsmith, clever
and punning in his power,   praised as 'Heorot'.
He broke no vow.   Bracelets he gave there,   80
treasure during feasting.   Towering was the structure –
high, horn-gabled –   but waiting for the huge surges
of hostile flame.   That future wasn't yet –
when the blade-hatred   of broken oaths
would wake, violent,   among vicious enemies.   85
   Jealously the unjust one,   enduring darkness,
suffered the daylight,   in dreary shadows:
a demon, each day   doomed to hear rejoicing,
the noise of the hall.   There was harp-music,
poet's clear-voiced song.   Who knew, recited,   90
told the creation   of earth for men,
said the Almighty   made the landscape,
eye-restful fields   enfolded by water;
set there, triumphant,   the sun and moon –
lights to illumine   land for its dwellers;   95
and decorated   the dales of ground

with tree-limbs, leaves;   life he also formed
and quick creatures   of every kind.
The tribe and their lord   lived in abundance,
most blessedly –   till one, their bane,   100
a hell-creature,   began his crimes.
He was named Grendel,   their wrathful guest,
infamous reiver   who ravened the moors –
wastelands, margins.   He'd remained a while
in the monstrous marsh,   a miserable half-man,   105
after the Lord banished him   among the bale of Cain's
dreadful kindred –   the dear justice
of the Almighty   for Abel's death.
Uncondoned, evil,   he was exiled by God
for that fell murder,   far from humanity.   110
From him are descended   all sin's offspring –
the monsters, the elves,   orc-corpses, carrion –
those misbegotten,   who contended with God
on time's causeway   until His requital.
The visitor crept,   after night's coming,   115
to the rearing walls,   saw how the Ring-Danes
were abandoned to rest   after their beer-party;
found there within   the force of the troop
asleep, unconcerned,   supped into stupor;
they were careless.   And the creature, unhallowed,   120
grim and greedy,   got himself ready
for savage cruelty –   and from their sleep then ripped
thirty warriors.   From there, like any predator
that's secured its prey,   he carried them home,
seeking his lair with   loot from the slaughter.   125
It was only at dawn,   at cracked daybreak,
that Grendel's cunning   became common knowledge,
and once it was confirmed,   a foment of cries
tore at the morning.   Motionless, Hrothgar –
beyond goodness now –   sat grief-stricken   130

among sorrow's surges.   No succour could be given
after they'd shown him   the shocking footprints
of their vicious guest.   Severe hardship,
hateful, endless –   hideous precedent,
since on successive nights   anew Grendel   135
committed atrocity,   untroubled, without conscience
for wrongdoing, evil;   he was too rapt in sin.
They slept afterwards   at a safe distance,
each choosing for himself   a separate bed
among distant rooms,   once the deadly malice   140
of the hall's occupant   was unsecret,
an overt hatred.   Evasion, then, escape –
they kept firmly   to far quarters.
So Grendel ruled,   an inglorious
one among many.   It stood empty at night   145
at last, the hall.   Those years were long:
their troubles he endured   for twelve winters,
the Scyldings' lord –   lost in miseries,
the country of sorrows.   And so it became known to
the children of men,   the mournful tale   150
no guarded story: Grendel contended
endlessly with Hrothgar,   enmity lasted
summer and winter,   sick violence,
turmoil, continual... And truce? Truce he
couldn't accept from   any son of the Danes,   155
wouldn't cease from malice   or settle for terms;
of the company, none   could expect compensation
for slain kinsmen   at their slayer's hands.
Pain – merciless,   remorseless – he caused.
Death's cunning shadow   over the adult and young   160
alike drifted;   darkness smothered
mist-shrouded moors,   and men couldn't say
when next, or how,   hell's malice would strike.
    And he kept committing   his crimes, hateful,

obsessed, malicious,   solitary in sin.   165
It was almost as if   all injuries
lived with him in Heorot,   hall hung with dark.
The Lord's mercy   he didn't merit, nor knew
the grace of His gifts   nor goodness or love:
an affliction he was, fierce,   a foe to all joys   170
in Hrothgar's mind.   Many often withdrew –
brave men, the best,   battle-hardened men –
to rune, to plan   how they could depose their foe
yet they were terrified   of his swift attacks.
They sometimes, too,   turned to images,   175
idols, tabernacles   of their ancient gods,
asked their devil for aid   against one whose deeds
had caused such distress.   Such was their custom, once:
it's how heathens hope –   hellish things in mind,
nestled in heart-deep.   How could they not know then   180
the Redeemer's deeds?   Not know the due owed God
in fitting praise –   the firmament's Helm,
its glorious One?   Woe, woe to those
who in shock and trouble   must shove their souls
into the fire's whelming,   forfeiting comfort   185
and hope of help!   Well-hallowed are those
who find after death   a Father's embrace,
who may in their Prince's care   and protection seek peace!
   They seethed, those sorrows –   seethed restlessly
in Hrothgar's mind.   Morning, daylight –   190
nothing brought relief.   Not the most wise liege-man
could avoid misery: severe were its griefs,
long-standing losses   lodged unshakably
in mind: evil;   mauling night-panic.
   Then, in those years of   this teeming world,   195
was a thane who heard – he was Hygelac's man,
a Geat, by repute good – of Grendel's crimes.
Rumour held him   to be hard, canny,

strongest among allies,   of a most able tribe.
A boat he had made,   best of wave-blades,   200
said that he'd seek out   sorrowing Hrothgar,
royal Hrothgar,   over the riven swan-road.
Nor did cooler heads   discount the idea
(though he was dear to them,   and for this new danger
they read omens   even as they encouraged him).   205
And then he hand-picked from   the people of the Geats
champions. The keenest   he chose, and at last
fifteen together   gathered by the gangplank
while he explained his plan   to pilot the coast.

Time passed, and held   the boat's passage,   210
rucking under cliff-falls.   They climbed into the prow
to watch tide-races   turbid with sand-bloom,
readied bright-polished   battle-treasures
in the ship's structure,   shoved off again –
on their mission intent,   menacing, purposed   215
on their enterprise   in their iron-bound boat.
Over the waves' pathways   wide-waked they came:
wind-cunning bird;   a wry-necked craft.
Soon, on the second   of successive days,
the crossing was done.   At the decorated   220
prow the watchman   pointed out the land,
the estranging slopes   of steep sea-cliffs,
nesses, headlands.   That hurtling voyage
was at an end.   And up they stood –
battle-troop of Weders   in a body jumping   225
gunwales, making fast   mere's-keel. Mail-shirts
grated, thrawn with effort. They gave thanks to God
for safe crossing   of the sundering tides.

On the cliff-top a   coast-guard, Scylding
lookout whose duty   was to relate news of   230
strangers and enemies,   seeing the stern war-gear
brought ashore – shield-boss,   shining battle-devices –,

determined to discover   who this company might be.
He came closer,   cannily, on horseback,
this thane of the king.   Clear-voiced, cautious   235
and with spear in hand   he spoke formally:
'What troop are you   who bring trappings of war –
'keen-bright byrnie   and keel's wave-blade –
'from your home's havens   here across the ocean,
'across the sea-currents?   I was sent holmwards   240
'to this kingdom's rim   as a coast-scout, guard
'of the sea-border,   so that no brutal aggression
'might trespass our land   from its outlying boundaries.
'And never have shield-guests   with unshattered battle-rims
'more brazenly arrived;   nor have you bothered to gain   245
'permission from the clan   and its mighty chiefs
'beforehand. There's been no consent.   Yet in your fine bearing
'and seeming lordliness   you're surely no mere
'feckless foot-soldier   in a frayed war-shirt.
'May your bearing   and your brazen face   250
'never come to mock you!   But nevertheless
'I here must ask   of your origins and coming:
'you won't follow further   into fair Dane-land
'unless you go as spies.   So, you spume-traveller,
'far-dweller, speak.   Frame your story   255
'to the point, plainly   and without posturing:
'where did you come from?   What caused your coming?'
    It was the oldest who   gave answer, unlocked
the sound store of   his subtle word-hoard:
'Of the gathered peoples   we're Geats by birth: 260
'Hygelac's hearth-troop,   hand-picked each one.
'My father had repute,   fame among this people:
'Ecgtheow his name,   a noble chief
'who outlasted many   mauling winters
'before time took him.   His reputation's kept   265
'to this day, known by   nigh-on everybody.

'We resolved to come   to seek your lord,
'Healfdan's great son,   with a high purpose.
'You can tell, I'm sure,   what's true and fitting.
'Our sworn errand   involves no slinking,   270
'but is a great duty   to your Danish king.
'It's a pressing matter,   too important to keep
'secret. So, tell us   if what they say is true,
'if what we heard is right.   Harm seems to sit
'among your people, hate   present at nightfall,   275
'made manifest in   manglings and vanishings –
'in humiliation.   It may well be
'that I can show Hrothgar,   generously and surely,
'how a properly laid   plan wisely made
'might overcome this foe – if fate indeed   280
'is ever to help, or change   hallow this evil –
'so that hate's whelming   will lose its heat.
'If not, then always   shall this most noble of halls
'stand in affliction,   endure distress
'forever, bereft   and racked in time.'   285
    On horseback he sat,   sea-rim's watchman,
and replied: 'It's plain   that purposes and words
'can differ. Every   dutiful officer
'knows that. Therefore   in this instance,
'given what I've heard of   your great loyalty   290
'to Hrothgar, I'll allow   your unharmed passage
'while you're armed, war-dressed.   Your way onwards
'I'll show you myself,   and as a surety I'll set
'some of our own forces   to fend off any
'thieves or looters   from the long-lined strakes,   295
'sand-grounded prow   of your paint-fresh ship
'until, coil-necked, this   craft and its cargo
'sail again to the Geats'   great weather-marches.
'Your will and courage   have caused me to think
'you'll survive any   vicious battle-rush.'   300

He bridled his horse.   The boat lay still.
It rode on its ropes,   a roomy vessel,
secure, anchored.   Boar's-crest glittered
over their cheek-guards;   fire-cherished, it protected
their lives, bolstered   in bright smith-flame.   305
They fretted to be off;   force hastened on:
they marched together   until they could glimpse it –
gold-hung timbers,   towering Heorot.
Among the mass of men,   of mighty halls
it was most fabled.   Majesty it held.   310
Its light carried   over the lands round it.
The battle-worthy   witness showed them
this great landmark   so they could gain the way,
these travellers from afar,   then turned on his horse,
edgy, careful,   calling over his shoulder: 315
'I must leave you.   May your Lord keep you
'and hold you in his grace,   grant you safety,
'sure journey's end.   Now, back to the shore,
'where vigilance awaits   violent intrusion.'
    The path was straight,   stone-paved; admitted   320
men walking together.   Their mail-shirts shone:
hardened, hand-crafted,   hoops of iron
sang in battle-dresses.   And so they'd appear
unthreatening in   all that war-gear
they set down their shields –   sea-weary travellers –   325
spell-burnished rims,   at the building's spur,
chose to enter,   chain-mail chiming,
all warrior-like.   Outside, their spears,
war-devices,   stood against a wall,
ash-wood upright   in air-grey dawn.   330
Custom was honoured.   Then came questions.
One fighter puzzled   at their purpose, origin:
'From where have you brought   these embossed shield-fronts,
'ash-grey armour,   artfully made helmets,

'these stocks for strife?   Understand that I'm   335
'Hrothgar's emissary.   I've hardly seen
'so many of a force   look so magnificent.
'It must be high spirits   speed you to Hrothgar –
'magnanimity, courage,   rather than exile's needs.'
He was answered by   battle's reputation,   340
by the Weders' chief,   whose words issued
resounding from his helmet: 'We're Hygelac's men
'and hearth-brothers.   Beowulf's my name.
'And certainly I shall tell   Healfdan's great son –
'your renowned leader –   the news I must.   345
'If he so wishes,   your ancestral chief,
'then we'll greet his honour   in good fashion.'
Wulfgar then spoke;   he was of Wendel stock;
winning integrity   in both wisdom and war
made his reputation tall: 'I'll tell Hrothgar,   350
'scion of Scyldings,   of what you so bluntly say,
'tell our treasure-giver   that you're petitioning him
'as far-travellers   to our fabled chief.
'His answer I'll return   as early as I can –
'whatever the reply   of our prince might be.'   355
He hurried away   to where Hrothgar sat –
aged, silver-haired,   among his set of men;
strong-framed Wulfgar   stood face-to-face,
capably courteous,   with the Danish king.
To his Scylding lord   he told his message: 360
'There are seamen outside   saying they're Geatish,
'come here from afar   over the water's fret.
'The most senior   of these so-sayers
'is called Beowulf,   who begs audience
'with you, lord king,   a request for speech   365
'and mutual esteem.   A straight answer
'I think they merit,   thrice-honoured Hrothgar.
'In their battle-gear,   in their bearing and manners

'they seem worthy,   and worthiest perhaps
'the resolute liegeman   who led them here.'   370
The Scyldings' helm,   Hrothgar, then spoke:
'I knew him well   when he was a wean, a boy!
'His father, his great   forebear was Ecgtheow,
'to whom Hrethel the Geat   gave his daughter
'in marriage: this man   of merit outside   375
'is their son, who'll find   friends here indeed.
'They've said, you know –   our sailors have said,
'those who carry coin-gifts   to the Geat coffers –
'that Beowulf's grasp   can grip as strong
'as thirty men!   His mettle's God-sent –   380
'it's God's kind grace   has given him to us,
'our clan, in this crisis,   our encounter with horror,
'with Grendel's hate –   and who doubts it?
'Well. He shall get treasure,   the good man, for
'his great daring.   And so go now, quick,   385
'bid welcome to   these brave travellers
'and tell the whole troop   they must turn inside
'and have as their own   the open-handedness
'of the Danish people!'   So to the hall-doorway
Wulfgar went off,   spoke words from its frame: 390
'The ever-powerful,   the lord of all
'Danes East and West,   knows your ancestry.
'Your resolve in crossing   the coiled sea-tides
'is welcome here,   to Hrothgar and to us,
'and you've been granted entrance   in that grim war-coat,   395
'those bold battle-masks,   at Hrothgar's bidding –
'but while speech is exchanged   let those shields and spears,
'steeled slaughter-gear,   stay here outside.'
   He stood, their chief,   straightened, and his chosen
soldiers stood round him.   Some stayed behind,   400
minding the armoury   as their commander asked,
while the rest went on,   directed on their way

under Heorot's roof.   Under his hard helm-crest
Beowulf entered   the bale-stricken hall,
spoke up bravely.   His byrnie shone,   405
a corselet worked   by the most cunning smith.
    'Hrothgar, hail to you!   I'm Hygelac's man,
'and of his tribe and troop.   Many times I've won
'renown over the years.   News of Grendel
'is hardly unknown   in my home country.   410
'Sailors told us   that this towering hall,
'best of strongholds,   was beset, unused
'by its gallant guardians   when evenings gather,
'when in heaven's vault   shadows find a home.
'And so I was advised by   those most virtuous and wise   415
'among my own people,   who of old know well
'my power, that I should purpose,   princely Hrothgar,
'to seek you out.   They've seen me return
'battle-stained from times   of blood, when I've been covered
'in foes' life-flow: five, once, I bound,   420
'five from a giant-race,   or in the waves' fury
'killed sea-monsters.   They saw no further dawn
'but drowned in the Weders'   deathly vengeance
'as our enemies merit.   And my meaning now
'is to take on Grendel,   this evil, this fiend,   425
'and do so alone.   Nonetheless, I ask
'of you, Dane-Bright,   that you yield to this
'sole need of mine, this single request.
'Scyldings' Storm-shelter,   Shaper, Protector,
'do not refuse me: now this far I've come,   430
'let me work alone,   or allow me help
'only from my comrades,   so I can cleanse Heorot.
'I found out also   that this fen-creature,
'rabid in recklessness,   won't use ready weapons.
'So I, too, shall scorn them – not scath of sword   435
'nor that great battle-rim,   the gold-edged shield –

'to gain further honour　for my fair-recalled
'lord, Hygelac.　With hand-grip alone
'I'll fight against this fiend,　force against force.
'God's doom is just,　whoever death takes there!　　440
'But if Grendel wins,　he'll want to glut himself,
'to gorge on Danes　in this glorious hall,
'unafraid and unchallenged,　as he feasted before
'on your gallant warriors.　No grave you'll need
'for me, in that case,　no corpse-coverings　　445
'or customs: carrion　I'll be, claimed by death,
'borne off from battle　in blood, a body
'he'll slaver on, swallow　without a second thought,
'frantic with greed in　his fouled moor-hole.
'There'll be no need then　for necessary rites,　　450
'no need for burial:　my body will be nothing.
'But if battle seize me　send to Hygelac
'this best war-shroud,　these shining links
'I wear, the work　of Wayland and a gift
'of Hrethel the Geat.　Fate goes as it must.'　　455
　　Hrothgar then spoke,　helm of Scyldings:
'For fame, for our defence,　my fair Beowulf,
'and for kindness' sake　you sought us out.
'Your father, you know –　the feud was most bitter –
'killed Heatholaf,　Heatholaf the Wulfing,　　460
'with his bare hands. No　bounty could be afforded,
'the tribe was afraid,　and so he took his leave,
'seeking the lands of　south-lying Danes,
'our ancestors,　over the arching waves.
'I was a youthful king,　a young chieftain　　465
'in those far-off days,　whose duty was to keep
'the kingdom rich.　And Heorogar, my kin,
'my father's first　and a fine brother,
'had died. He was a better,　better man than I.
'But it had to be paid, the price　of that princely feud.　　470

'Over the water's heave   to the Wulfings I sent
'fame-ancient treasures.   Your father in return
'swore me loyalty.   But now sorrow comes on –
'fear, though it shames me   to have to confess it
'to anyone... to you.   With his avid hatred,   475
'with his never-glutted envy,   Grendel's attacks
'have made Heorot waste.   Warriors are vanishing:
'fate sweeps them off   into his foul clutches.
'May God after all   some help grant us
'in this foul folly!   With filled ale-cups   480
'they boasted into their beer,   my best fighters:
'how they intended to wait   in this weathered mead-hall,
'meet Grendel's wrath   with ravening blades.
'But when dawn whitened,   when daybreak came,
'blood-havoc was hung   in the hall again,   485
'bench-planks ran red,   rancid with slaughter,
'and I had fewer left   of my beloved tribe.
'My trusted warriors   were taken by death.
'But sit, sit now   and let your senses rest
'while tales are told   of true courage.'   490
    Bench-space was cleared   in that baleful hall
so that the Geat soldiers   could sit together.
They came forward,   fair-set fighters,
proud of their power.   The mead-flagon passed,
wrought cups were filled   by a watchful slave.   495
Meanwhile one sang,   sweetly, clear-voiced –
Heorot's hall-poet –   until in that unhallowed place
the garrison revelled,   Geat and Dane together.
Unferth then spoke –   Ecglaf's offspring,
who crouched at the feet   of the Scylding king.   500
There Beowulf's bane   unburdened his spite,
despised the newcomer,   displeasing many.
(His envy wouldn't allow   any other man
on middle-earth   to be more valued,

more rated under the heavens,   than he himself.)   505
    'Are you that Beowulf –   Breca's opponent?
'You contended at swimming   in the salt wave-fall,
'foolhardy, trying   tide-run, sea-face,
'risking danger   in deep water,
'besotted with pride.   Dissuade you two?   510
'Neither friend nor foe,   when you fared the torrents,
'could convince you   of your rash vanity.
'A sorry business!   The sea you clasped,
'plunged through with hand-strokes,   those pale sea-paths,
'yawed in wave-yell   while the yellow breakers   515
'surged with winter.   Seven nights you hung
'in the callous waters.   And he overcame you –
'had the more power.   As another morning broke,
'sea disgorged him   on the Raumar's sands
'and he turned for home,   his ancestral turf,   520
'land of the Brondings,   his beloved people,
'their fair strongholds.   Family he had there,
'property; possessions.   His promise beat yours:
'by Beanstan's son   you were bested.
'What confidence, then –   despite rumour's clang,   525
'big-noised Beowulf   at battle's onset –
'could I drag up now   that you'd dare Grendel's
'night-shadowed approach?   I expect the worst.'
    Beowulf, Ecgtheow's   offspring, then spoke:
'My dear Unferth…   Are you drunk, over-aled,   530
'that you should speak of Breca's   spirit and journey
'so spitefully?   It's a sure truth that
'I, ocean-strong,   had an easier power
'among the waves' hurling   than…whomsoever.
'We two, you know,   way back in childhood,   535
'had once boasted –   we were both then still
'green and growing –   that we'd go, miles out,
'onto the quickening sea.   And that we accomplished.

'We had a bare sword-blade –   burnished, hand-heavy –
'which we carried swimming.   (It was the coming of whales   540
'we wanted to prevent.)   No wave, no tide
'prised him yet from me,   no puling current,
'subtle undertow… Nor would I leave him.
'As if we were stitched together   on that storm-stirred sea
'we swam five nights all told,   until a malevolent tide,   545
'dangerous combers,   then drove us apart.
'It was coldest weather.   We were caught out there
'in darkening night,   north-griping wind,
'steep-sided waves,   a stricken ocean.
'It was the ring-hardened   rigs of my corselet   550
'provided defence   against vicious sea-monsters –
'interlocked chain-links   lay, touched with gold,
'protecting my body.   One battle-mottled
'sea-serpent I   seized, dragged it down;
'a grim death-grip.   It was granted me,   555
'as the beast still writhed,   to bury the sword
'in its forehead, destroy   by force of my hand
'that lashing animal   and its livid onrush.
     'There were further attacks.   Tested often
'by these loathsome things,   I relieved them of time   560
'with my trusted sword –   as was entirely fitting.
'They took no joy   in the turn of fate,
'those revolting beings,   obliged to receive me
'at their monstrous wakes   on the mere's bottom;
'and the next morning,   maimed by swords'-play,   565
'they lay swollen   on the shoreline's sands,
'slain by blade-fury,   so that in those buttressed fjords
'sea-travellers would never   afterwards think twice
'about what underlay their path.
                              Light flamed the east,
'God's bright beacon;   the boiling of the sea   570
'subsided. Here   I could see headlands,

'wind-battered cliff-walls...   If his courage is good,
'destiny will cherish   its chosen warrior.
'So it happened   that my sword's keen edge
'killed nine monsters,   and never was there told   575
'of a harder fight   under the heavens' wheeling,
'in a night's skirmish,   in a scathing tide,
'of a more hard-pressed fighter.   Yet my power and grip
'granted me safety   and the sea bore me
'exhausted in its flood   to the Finns' homeland   580
'on surging tides.
    Have I heard anyone tell
'of you, Unferth,   any such battle-feat,
'bruted sword-bale?   Even Breca never –
'no, neither of you –   in the noise of battle
'performed a deed   as dangerous as that   585
'with etched sword-blade –   you think I boast too much? –
'nor would, were you to battle   your brothers' slayer,
'one who harms your kin.   It's in hell, Unferth,
'your bravery will be judged –   however big your brains.
'I say truly,   son of Ecglaf,   590
'that Grendel would never   have visited such grim,
'humiliating crimes   on Heorot's majesty
'if your doom and courage   had been as dauntless,
'fierce, as durable   as you dare to claim.
'And yet he's discovered   he doesn't have to care! –   595
'hasn't learnt to dread   lashing sword-tumult
'from those vicious victims,   those "victors" the Danes!
'He extracts his toll,   treats all your folk
'to no mercy,   mangles where he pleases,
'slays, sends to death,   receiving no return   600
'from Danish spears.   I'll dare show him
'Geatish courage,   combat's clamour,
'minded to offer him   mettled opposition.
'Again may you all go   to the good mead-cup

'when another sunrise   in swept radiance   605
'chases southerly   over the children of men!'
   Then the grey-haired king,   the giver of treasures,
was glad: Bright-Danes   from Beowulf himself,
powerful captain,   had heard his keen purpose,
could count on his courage.   And so the clans feasted: 610
there was men's laughter,   a mess of noise,
words of banter.   Wealhtheow appeared –
she was Hrothgar's queen,   skilled in custom,
courtesies – and greeted   each of those good warriors.
She shimmered in gold.   The shining cup   615
she passed to Hrothgar first,   famed protector
of the East-Danes,   urged him to enjoy it,
to drink deeply.   Dear to his people
he partook smiling,   that time-hallowed king,
of feast, hall-cup.   Then the Helming queen,   620
radiant in jewels,   passed around the hall,
offering everyone –   both old and young –
the shining bowl,   until it was Beowulf
at last she reached   in rare spirits.
To the Geat chieftain   her chosen words   625
were wise, thoughtful.   She gave thanks to God
for fulfilling her prayers   for a fighting man,
a comfort for their pains.   As he took the cup
boldly from Wealhtheow,   Beowulf spoke out,
eager for battle,   for blood's onrush.   630
And Ecgtheow's son   said these words there:
'When I set out on   the slopes of the sea,
'sat in that vessel   with my vaunting band,
'my purpose was clear: to do your people's will
'or to die doing it   in the demon's clutch.   635
'And so to the utmost   of earl-like courage
'I'll carry that out,   or in carnage die,
'here take my end –   here, in Heorot.'

47

The woman liked those   well-chosen words,
that promising speech.   Well-pleased, she turned –   640
stately, gold-clothed –   to sit with her lord.
    And like an old memory   that mighty hall
rang again with noise,   with gallant laughter,
a people at ease,   until presently
Healfdan's great son   would seek his bed,   645
sleep after supper.   He sensed the killer
intended some attack   on the towering hall,
had planned all day,   from pluming dawn
to the unshaken shadows   of sure night-fall,
to come looming   from the lost darkness,   650
black drowned in black.
                         They bade goodnight.
The king and Beowulf   while the company stood
took leave of each other,   wished luck and health.
Hrothgar gave charge   of the hall to Beowulf,
saying these final words: 'Never once before,   655
'never since I could lift a shield   aloft with my hands,
'have I left control of   this towering Dane-hall
'to anyone – except you.   This most excellent house
'have now and hold,   and your high purpose
'remember on your watch.   All you might ever wish for   660
'is yours if you come   from this conflict living.'
    Then Hrothgar left.   Lord of the Scyldings
with his war-like troop   turned from the mead-hall.
The old war-chief   sought Wealhtheow, his queen
and his bed-mate.   Abroad it was known   665
that the Glory-King   had set a guard in Heorot
against Grendel's wrath,   a rare watchman
against monsters' spite – that was a special office,
a duty given   by the Danish lord.
The Geat-born man   had the greatest trust   670
in his own courage,   the kindness of the Lord.

He took off his   iron corselet,
helmet, wrought battle-sword,   best of weapons'-kind,
ordered an attendant   to guard those trappings,
and before he went to bed   Beowulf from goodness   675
spoke out bravely,   boastful, taunting:
'I count myself no less   keen for battle,
'grim, blood-lustful,   than Grendel himself.
'No sword I'll take   to his neck for killing,
'to prise him from life,   proper though that would be.   680
'He knows nothing   of the noble arts,
'reciprocal play   of sword or shield,
'though he's renowned for   unnatural force.
'And so tonight, no blades.   Unburdened, unarmed
'we must face each other,   if he can force himself   685
'to fight without weapons.   Far-seeing God
'will afterwards judge   in his great justice
'who'll gain glory,   whichever the gainer is.'
He pressed his cheek   on the pillow, this man
of courage. He lay   among his keen-hearted   690
shipmates. None could know   for sure that they'd ever
be able to seek   their ancestral place,
shining homeland,   their sheltering sky.
They'd heard, after all,   that evil, death
had worked in that hall   to haul from life   695
too many of the Danes.   But for the Geat-born men
the Lord, weaving   wonderful destiny,
determined they'd take   triumph out of time.
Through one man's power   they'd all come through.
Truly it's spoken   that the Spirit of God   700
rules eternal   in the times of men,
for ever and ever.   Out of darkness
he came sliding,   slipping from shadows.
The warriors were slack,   slept on guard-duty…

all but one of them.   Of old it was known   705
that the sin-scather   couldn't drag them into the shadows
if God forbade it.   And in the bated dark
one man, watchful,   waited in anger
for battle to begin,   blood running with wrath.
    Out of the moorland,   falls of mist-slopes,   710
cursed, shunned by God,   Grendel came walking.
This ravager meant   to harm menfolk,
entrap them by trickery   in the towering hall.
This cloud-walker   came to the building,
and plain in his sight   were the plastered walls   715
plaited with gold-work.   It wasn't his beginning –
he'd sought Hrothgar's   homestead before –
but never before,   never afterwards
did he find harder luck   among the hall's guardians.
So, joy-deprived,   this journeying man   720
came to the fortress.   Forged metal hinges
on the door gave way,   as soon wrecked as touched.
He broached, hostile,   hall's cavernous mouth,
intent, enraged.   Too soon afterwards
the fiend tread-marked   the tile-scrolled floor,   725
in ire came on.   In his eyes flickered
something like firelight,   flames of hatred.
A gathering of men   his gaze compassed:
band of kinsmen;   brothers' bedchamber;
brave thanes… asleep.   His bent heart laughed.   730
Before another daybreak,   his due was to part
each one's body from life.   Livid, he exulted:
fury had found them   after their feasting,
his prey…But now   it was no longer
his fate, after that night,   to fillet, rip at   735
more men-children.   Mighty eyes there –
Hygelac's kinsman –   weighed his horrible intent,
the surge of will,   the sudden attack.

Grendel's brutality   brooked no delay:
as his first foray   his fist enclosed   740
a sleeping guard, greedily tore him.
He bit muscles,   drank blood from veins,
swallowed gobs of bone.   Soon he'd eaten
all of the corpse-flesh –   all of it, even
feet, limp fingers.   He went forward, approached,   745
tried to seize another   of the sane and living,
to wrest him from sleeping…   He reached out in turn,
sat up the same moment,   sensing malice,
held hostility   in a huge hammer-lock.
That brew of crimes   discovered instantly   750
that never on middle-earth   had his knowing met
a mightier grip   from any mortal,
nor anywhere under heaven.   He was uneasy,
was sickened by fear;   none sooner would flee.
Frit mind, shaken…   Shadows he longed for,   755
concourse with devils.   But his destiny now
lay not in living   as in the long-before.
Then Hygelac's thane   thought, and worthily,
of his speech that night,   stood spear-upright
and fastened his grip.   Fingers shattered there…   760
the creature was fleeing…   then closer came the man…
However, wherever,   the wicked demon
wished only to escape   unscathed, and from there
vanish into remoteness,   yet his vicious fingers
were in a remorseless grasp… Grievous, the journey   765
to Heorot that harm   had had to make!
Hall-timbers dinned.   Among the Danes there,
each of the men who   manned the stronghold,
there was desperate terror.   Tearing anger
filled both fighters;   the frame of the hall   770
resounded – miraculous   that its rafters stood
fury's combat,   that it didn't fall to earth,

such a fair structure;   but it was strengthened
inside and out   with iron shackles
forged skilfully.   (Yet its furnishings,   775
gathered mead-benches   with their gold cladding,
battered from their bases   while the bale played out –
or so I've heard rumoured.)   Could they ever have reckoned,
the Scylding witan   with their wise counsels,
that their splendid hall,   hung with antlers,   780
could threaten to shatter,   be shaken by cunning –
unless fire swallowed it?   But now fury was sound –
new, unfamiliar.   North-Danish guards,
defending positions   on the furthest wall,
were fixed by fear,   hearing failure's song,   785
the ghoul-crying   of God's enemy,
his song of defeat,   the furious lament
of hell's inmate,   still held in the grip
of the man whose power,   whose might was strongest
at that time in   this transitory world.   790
By no means did   the men's guardian
intend to leave the   terror-bringer alive,
nor perpetuate   that pointless life
among any other people.   And their ancestral swords
Beowulf's followers   began to brandish: 795
wherever, however,   he who was able
was required to defend   his captain's life.
As they took to the combat   they couldn't know,
resolute warriors   wanting to rain blows on
every side, striving   to seek the life   800
of their un-souled enemy,   that their sin-stricken
foe had rendered   wrought iron's blades
everywhere useless,   so that no earthly weapon,
war-pike could ever   cause him any injury.
At that time in   this time-stricken world   805
his parting from life   had to take place in

a more wretched manner,   and his maimed spirit be
exiled into misery,   Otherworld's malice.
He once had in mind   murder, affliction,
mutilation   among men-folk –   810
time's reprobate,   who contended with God.
But now he discovered   his skin could perish:
Hygelac's kinsman,   hard, implacable,
was tightening his grip.   The two, while alive,
were a torment to each other: it was agony of body   815
Grendel suffered there.   In his shoulder appeared
a sudden wound-gape: sinews tore apart
and cartilage burst.   It was to Beowulf
battle was granted.   And Grendel fled,
mortal, wounded,   to the mist-havens,   820
his friendless dwelling,   fearing certainty's
end, and the ending   of all his life,
his numbered days.   The Danes' wishes
had been fulfilled   in fury and blood.
The salt-traveller had   saved, purified   825
Hrothgar's fair hall.   With heart-deep courage
he'd held it whole   against hatred. Now
he smiled, happy with   such sure night-work.
The Geat leader   had his late promise
to the Danes fulfilled: to redeem the malice,   830
the grief they'd undergone,   the great hardships
they'd had to endure,   heart-savage troubles.
A sure token   he showed, displaying
hand, arm, shoulder –   the huge compass
of Grendel's grip –   together, a blood-mass   835
he set on high   under Heorot's roof.
    As I heard it said,   the same morning
brought many a thane   to the massive gift-hall –
near or distant   neighbours arrived,
clansmen and chieftains,   to see the carnage-trace,   840

monstrous foot-prints.   Few who saw them
regretted his going,   his unglutted flight,
his exhausted trail –   urgent, defeated –
back to his mere-nest,   overmastered by battle.
Doomed, driven away,   to his dire fenland   845
he returned, trailing   a track of gore.
There was his mere-pit –   it moiled with blood.
Waves rucked and swilled,   swirled restlessly
on battle-memory,   blood-wallowings, bone.
And in there at last he hid,   where hatreds seethed.   850
Unredeemed, dying   under those dismal wastes
lay his heathen soul.   And hell took it.
    On their roan horses   they rode away –
youths and veterans,   in victory's pride.
From the mere they turned,   tall in their courage: 855
bone-men, war-horses.   Beowulf's deeds were
told over again.   Continually it was said
that south or north   across sundering sea,
earth's great expanse   or spread of heaven,
there was nowhere a better   to brandish a shield,   860
no-one more right   to rule kingdoms.
And in this clamour they   included Hrothgar,
found no fault in   such a noble king.
    Sometimes that brave   battle-band allowed
their bay horses   to break into a gallop,   865
to race where the tracks   turned easiest,
were known to be sound.   Sometimes a thane –
custom-laden,   who recalled the songs
and all and more   of the ancient ways –
made new words from   his knowledge of the old,   870
set them truly.   He began to recite –
best, most skilful –   Beowulf's doings,
spinning out his song   in the subtlest way,
well-varied words.   And well-nigh all

he'd heard said of   Sigmund's deeds too   875
he repeated, deeds   of prowess, far
wanderings, stories   that had been witnessed by few,
so that men's children   had no measure of them,
the feuds, the crimes,   except Fitela,
nearby as always   when his uncle inclined   880
to tell such tales,   since the two were close
comrades, friends in   every conflict:
they'd felled many of   monstrous giant-kin
with their swords' edges.   Around Sigmund grew,
after his death-day,   some dazzling tales: 885
how by sheer courage   he'd killed a dragon,
treasure-hoard's keeper.   He'd crept alone
under the ash-stained stone,   young and easy-skilled,
on his fierce venture,   without Fitela for once.
And so it happened   that his sword punctured   890
the plated scales –   its point right through
to the wall. The dragon   died there thrashing.
Such a great hero   had gained for himself
the right to enjoy,   as he judged most fit,
those ornaments, treasures.   He tricked out a ship,   895
that son of Wæls,   with the wonderful loot.
And in its dire heat-throes   the dragon melted.
    He was the most widely known   of the world's heroes:
all nations knew   of this renowned fighter
and how protective   was his untainted power.   900
He thrived of old,   after Heremod's
dark might declined,   was caught by force
by giants, betrayed   and duly killed.
Heremod was given to   heart-whelming sorrows,
for too long was   a terrible grief   905
to his court and kin.   Countless times then
they'd lamented his fall,   friends and counsellors,
those who'd once trusted   in his protection,

saw him as a royal son,   successor to his father,
bulwark against troubles,   a true guardian   910
of strongholds, treasures,   Scyldings' home-turf.
(Such a one was Beowulf,   the best beloved,
Hygelac's kinsman,   the kindest of friends.)
Yet wickedness   waited for Heremod:
sin possessed him   and received him.   915
  Down dawn-flanked tracks   they drove their mounts.
Meanwhile, morning   mustered into brightness.
Many a fighting-man   came to the mead-hall,
high-gabled house,   hugely curious
to see such a wonder.   Hrothgar himself,   920
treasure-hoard's keeper,   with a troop round him,
walked from Wealhtheow's   and her women's rooms –
good, kingly it was –   and together with his queen
and her attendants pressed   down the path hallwards.
  When he'd arrived at   the rich weavings   925
of Heorot's huge,   high-gabled roof,
he stood on its steps   and stared upwards
to where Grendel's claw   hung among the gold-work.
He spoke: 'May endless thanks   go to the All-Wielder,
'to God, for this sight!   From Grendel I had my fill   930
'of stricken griefs, yet   God can always
'shape miracles,   Shepherd of his flock.
'Not even yesterday   there was no-one, I thought,
'in the wide world who   such woe could lessen
'or remedy the wrong   when this royal house stood   935
'battered and blood-stained,   when the best warriors
'of the witan imagined   such woe endless,
'not knowing, all their lives,   how to outlast, protect
'against the shuck-bodied evil,   the shining wraith
'striking our garrison.   Now God's given one man   940
'the power to finish   what all our fine planning
'couldn't accomplish.   Whoever carried this one

'in her belly, gave birth   to him in the brood of men,
'may say, if she still lives,   that the Lord Everlasting
'chose her for favour   at her child-bearing.   945
'And now, Beowulf,   best beloved and
'the best of men: I mean to adopt
'and love you as a son: see that you keep this
'new kinship well.   Nothing, nothing you'll lack
'of the world's riches   while I still wield power.   950
'Often I've honoured   a less able man,
'have given treasure   to the less than great,
'to lesser fighters.   But it shall live, your fame –
'made by your courage, by   merits in action –
'for ever and ever.   May the All-Wielder   955
'give you his due always,   as He has done just now!'
    And Ecgtheow's son,   Beowulf, then said,
'With great favour   I fought, struggled
'though trials of courage,   contended the strength
'of an unknown enemy.   If anything I'd have preferred   960
'for you yourself   to have been able to see
'that devil, death-stricken   in his doomed trappings.
'I thought to grapple him   in his gore-filled bed,
'bind and clasp him   in a brutal grip
'so he'd lie sweltering   and not elude me,   965
'not slip away.   Since it was unwished by God
'that couldn't be done: I couldn't prevent
'his last escape.   He limped away,
'couldn't be held fast in   my firmest of grips.
'He was monstrous strong.   Yet for a memory   970
'he left behind his hand,   huge-muscled arm.
'Reft and wretched,   no remedy that bought
'for such a beaten soul.   His baleful life –
'soiled, sin-stricken –   didn't stretch the more,
'and now his wound wastes him,   an unwilling suture,   975
'ever-bloodied bandage.   And so he must abide judgement,

'broken and bleeding.   He'll be brought at last
'to the great justice   of the most glittering Lord,
'who will deem truly   what such a time-stained sinner
'has merited, in His   manifold justice.'   980
   So too Unferth,   son of Ecglaf,
stood in silence –   no sordid boasts
now that they'd seen Beowulf's   success for themselves:
blood-freaked hand hanging   from the braid-tiled roof,
monstrous fingers.   Fronting each was   985
a streaked spur, like   a steel-tipped nail:
the heathen's hard   and heinous talon.
Everyone said that   no iron or blade,
however tempered   or time-hallowed,
could have bested, harmed   that bloodied battle-hand.   990
   Then the order was given   that the great garrison
was to be decked, that hands   should decorate Heorot:
men and women both   were busy, tricking out
the hall. Hangings,   gold-chased tapestries,
glittered on stonework,   and they were astonished, all   995
who stared up there: outstanding it was.
Yet not long before,   the lovely hall-yard
had been smashed, broken.   Smith-work, iron hinge
lay ripped apart   and it was the roof, only,
the remained sound when   the sin-creature,   1000
despairing of his life,   sped away fleeing
in his stricken guilt.   Extinction's flight,
and whatever his merits,   is easy for no man
but all the same each soul   must seek out, each
of all earth-dwellers,   each daughter and son,   1005
the prepared place where   their present bodies,
sealed in their death-bed,   shall be set to sleep
after life's feasting.
             Time forged onwards:
Healfdan's great son   would go to the hall,

to share himself   in the shining feast.   1010
No clan have I heard   better carry themselves
about their getter of treasure   in a bigger gathering.
And so to the bench they bent,   blessed survivors,
relishing revelry –   rim-bright mead-cups
and many of them.   Kinsmen of old –   1015
Hrothgar and Hrothulf –   were in high spirits
in the raftered hall.   Heorot was filled with
friends and allies.   Freak-runed treachery
hadn't yet forced itself   on the Scylding folk.
A golden banner   to Beowulf was given   1020
by Healfdan's son –   sign of triumph;
and many saw there,   set before Beowulf,
bright battle-standard,   byrnie and helmet,
great treasure-sword.   From the teeming flagon
Beowulf drank deep.   For this due reward,   1025
renowned gifting,   there was no need for shame.
Nor have I ever heard fabled   any four treasures –
all gold-gleaming –   given by many
more graciously   across the mead-benches.
And that helmet!   Around its high-set crest   1030
a head-guard, metalled,   held death distant
so that no file-hardened,   savage forcing
could harm its sure temper   when the shield-wielder
had to fight against   the fiercest of foes.
Eight horses then   Hrothgar commanded   1035
brought to the hall-floor.   They were bridled with gold,
led from the courtyard.   One carried as it stood
a gem-studded saddle,   jewel-encrusted.
That was the battle-seat   of the best of kings:
Healfdan's great son   sat there at sword-clash,   1040
always in the vanguard,   in victory's press,
his skill legend   in the scath of death.
And on Beowulf then   both treasures were

bestowed: the steeds,   the steel-chased weapons.
Hrothgar, Ingwin-Friend,   urged Beowulf to   1045
enjoy them well.   Justly, manly-wise,
the hoard-warden,   heroes' leader,
paid for the battle-rush   in proper terms,
in horses and arms.   Anyone could tell
no fault could be found   in such a fair bargain.   1050
And to every and each   of the earl-like heroes
who with Beowulf travelled   on the brine-spattered crossing
he gave many treasures   on those mead-benches –
most ancient relics –   and thus one man quit
with generous gold   all Grendel's crimes.   1055
(They would have been more   but for a witting God
shaping man-fate,   and one man's fierce courage.
All affairs of men   the Fate-Measurer
deemed and determined,   as He does today.
Understanding this,   to take stern forethought,   1060
is everywhere best.   For a man must abide
both brutal and blessed   in his brush with time.)
   There were supple song-lines,   sounding together
before Healfdan's son   and sword-leader.
Then the harp was plucked   and Hrothgar's scop   1065
was called to turn   a true story,
tell the mead-benches   a much-told tale:
of Hnaef Scylding,   hero of Half-Danes,
suddenly felled, with   Finn's sons and heirs,
in fierce fighting   against the Frisian host.   1070
Nor could Hildeburh   there bear to praise
good faith of foes: she was guiltless, lost
her beloved kin   at the linden-clash –
fair son and brother.   They were felled by Fate,
met with spear-wounds.   She mourned, that woman.   1075
And not wholly in vain   did Hoc's daughter
grieve creation   in that gallows dawn,

when she could witness   under the cloud-sway
kinsmen murdered –   the most-loved, once,
of her worldly joys.   War took away   1080
all but a few of   Finn's battle-thanes:
depleted in   that place of strife
he couldn't end   conflict with Hengest
nor clear the rest   of the remnant force
of Hnaef from their place.   Hengest made terms: 1085
another hall-space –   high throne and floor –
should be cleared for them;   they should keep, control,
own half of it   with their enemies' offspring;
and at the fee-gifting   Folcwalda's son
should then daily   honour the Danes,   1090
Hengest's clansmen,   in kind treat them
at the ring-giving,   getting and keeping
of plated gold,   just as his own people
would gain rewards,   gifts in the beer-hall.
And so they struck a truce,   the two parties,   1095
a firm peace-pledge.   Finn earnestly
swore Hengest oaths,   saying he'd honour,
with due advice,   the doomed remnant
of the earlier fight,   unless any man
were to dash the truce   by deed or word   1100
or undermine it   by malice or cunning –
even though Fate had   forced them to follow
their lord's slayer   when they'd been left lordless;
and if any Frisian   spoke falsely there,
reminding others   of the murderous feud,   1105
then the matter would end   on edges of swords.
The oath was sworn.   Old-won gold was
unbound from the hoard.   The best Scylding
battle-man lay ready   on the readied bale-wood.
Sweat-stained mail-shirt;   gold swine-symbol;   1110
iron-hard boar-crest: they were easily seen

on that funeral pyre,   whose prince had destroyed
so many with wounds   in well-known killings.
And there at Hnaef's burning   Hildeburh ordered
her son also   to be offered to flames,   1115
his body's vessel   to burn on the bier.
She mourned her boy   and his uncle both,
keened the sorrow-songs.   The crying climbed
to the sky like smoke,   scattered in flame-crackle
on that mighty barrow.   Heads melted there,   1120
bone-wounds burst open,   blood flowed away
from body's hate-bite.   Brute fire – greediest
of guests – ate all   of the gathered war-corpses
of both peoples.   Their best was gone.

    Newly friendless,   the Frisian men   1125
took themselves homeward,   travelled back to Friesland,
to their home places.   Yet Hengest still
stayed on with Finn   that stricken winter,
in utter misery,   remembering his land
though the dear-ringed prow   couldn't be driven seawards   1130
and the wave-holm boiled   in bitter storm,
tide strove with wind;   waves with winter
thickened, were ice-locked   until the thaw came on
and another spring   renewed the earth-yards –
as it still does now,   when unrestrained brightness   1135
drives spring ever on.   Ice hurries away,
earth's dress is fair,   each exile, each guest
thinks of his birthland.   But in the thaw Hengest
thought of vengeance rather than voyaging,
whether he could bring about   some bitter meeting   1140
when he could offer iron   to his enemies' sons.
And so, back home,   when Hunlafing
laid the bright-edged blade –   best of weapons,
and known among giants –   on his knees, he knew
not to refuse or break   that most fateful oath.   1145

And so Finn received   the sword-onslaught,
eager blood-foe,   in his own stronghold:
both gnawed by regret   for the earlier feud,
Guthlaf and Oslaf   over the ocean crossed
to lament such ills;   that maddened Finn's   1150
unresting mind;   and then his mead-hall was
reddened with foe-blood,   Finn put to death –
a king among his kin –   and his queen taken.
Scylding archers   to their ships carried
all the belongings   of that land's ruler,   1155
all they could find there   in Finn's stronghold:
seared jewels, gems.   Then across the sea's pathway
the royal bondswoman   was brought back to Denmark
and her true people.
                          The tale was told,
court poet sung out.   Sound swayed again   1160
along the beer-benches.   Bearers brought goblets –
wondrous, wine-beaded.   Then Wealhtheow walked,
glittering, gold-necklaced,   to where the good pair sat,
uncle and nephew,   each then still loyal,
still true to the other.   Unferth, court-spokesman,   1165
also sat there at the feet of his lord.   (His loyalty they thought
they trusted then, and his great courage,   though to his kin he
                                              was never
honourable in the clash of swords.)   The Scylding queen spoke:
'This brimful glass   receive, my giver
'of treasure, heart-lord.   Be happy. Be happy,   1170
'gold-friend of men,   and to the Geats speak in
'mild, fitting words,   as any man now should.
'Remember to give freely,   gladly to the Geat-men
'those gifts you've had   from both near and far.
'Someone told me   you'd take this warrior   1175
'as an adopted son.   The dear-bright hall
'Heorot's been blood-cleansed: its great blessings

'enjoy while you can.   When you're claimed by Fate
'and make your last journey,   leave to your kinsmen
'the kingdom and its clan.   Of kind Hrothulf   1180
'I'm sure: our kin   he'll keep and hold
'in honour if you,   most honoured Scylding,
'should die before him,   undone to the world.
'Our children I think   he'll choose to repay
'with everything good   when he gathers to mind   1185
'former favours,   when we furthered his fame
'when he was still youthful –   a stripling, a boy.'
Back to the benches,   to her own boys she turned –
Hrethric and Hrothmund,   and other heroes' sons,
sitting together.   And with them sat   1190
Beowulf, next to   those two brothers.
    The brimful cup   was borne to him, words
encouraged him to sup.   Sweet-wound gold was
offered graciously –   two arm-bracelets,
rings and garments   and a great necklace   1195
(heaviest of all I've   heard the earth can give).
Not from the treasure-hoard of   heroes was there better
offered under heaven,   not since Hama took
the bright-jewelled   torc of the Brosings
to the battle-burnished   township. It was the bitterness   1200
of Eormanric he fled,   choosing endless honour.
Swerting's grandson,   the Geat Hygelac,
wore that necklace   on his worst, last raid:
under his fierce banner   he defended all
treasure, slaughter-spoils.   Time carried him off: 1205
Fate forced his pride   to feuding, misery,
fighting with Frisians.   The fretted gem-stones
as ornament he wore   over the waves' brimming –
lustrous chief, who failed   under the linden-rush.
His remains then fell   into Frankish hands –   1210
the body-armour   and the bright jewel –

and lesser warriors   looted the corpses
after battle's shearing.   The Geatish bodies
filled a corpse-field... Acclaim filled Heorot.
Wealhtheow then spoke   before the warlike clans: 1215
'My best Beowulf,   use this bright necklace
'well, and this corselet: may they cause you pleasure.
'They're a nation's wealth: may your name always
'prosper in power.   Be patient, kind
'to your clansmen.   Your courage I won't forget.   1220
'What you've done here   will be doomed in praise
'from far and near   whatever men first may praise,
'will be known surely as   sea's width surrounds
'wind-yards, cliff-walls.   And so while you carry life
'be happy, prince. My   heart wishes you well,   1225
'and rich in treasures.   To my two sons be
'kind and careful,   a keeper of what's good.
'Here every man   is loyal to others,
'generous-minded,   and just to their lord.
'The clansmen are agreed,   the company readied.   1230
'They have drunk, promised,   and will do what's asked.'
    To the throne she went.   Thorough was the feasting.
The men drank deep.   Their doom they didn't know,
their grim destiny   (that has doomed others,
many an earl of old)   after evening fell   1235
and Hrothgar had left   the hall for rest
in his own quarters.   Countless times before
had a numberless band   slept in the beer-hall.
The benches were cleared,   the floor covered
with bolsters, bedding.   One beer-drinker,   1240
already doomed,   dossed in the hallway.
By their bedsteads they set   battle-scarred shield-rims,
shining linden,   and surely to be seen
over each warrior   on the old hall-floor
was a war-steeped helm,   war-ringed chain-mail   1245

and many a cruel spear.   It was their custom:
they were always ready   in the arts of war –
ready just the same   whether out raiding
or back at home,   as their bond-lord
well might determine.   They were a willing company.   1250
    They settled to sleep.   Certainly one there
was to owe for napping,   as had often happened
when Grendel stalked   the stricken gold-hall,
practised, unrighteous,   until his rightful end,
his criminal's death.   And it was claimed widely,   1255
had even been seen,   that a second still lived:
second avenger,   survivor who'd outlived
the grievous fight: Grendel's mother –
she-troll, monster –   mind full of loss,
forced to survive in   fierce water-depths,   1260
in the cold currents,   after Cain's exile
when his sword's keen edge   killed his own brother,
his father's child.   He fled, blood-stained
and murder-marked,   left man's company,
haunted the wastelands.   That awoke a host   1265
of exiled ghosts –   and Grendel was one,
hate-filled, accursed,   who at Heorot found
a wakeful watchman   witness his coming.
Matched, close-gripped, were   the monster and the man,
but the man drew on   the might given him –   1270
most generous of gifts –   and ordained by God.
In the great Wielder's   grace he trusted,
His comfort and aid,   and thus aided, slew
the foul hell-wraith.   He too fled the place,
saw, dream-emptied,   the sad death-dwellings.   1275
He was man's enemy.   Yet his mother also
in gallows-minded   greed intended
to make her harrowed visit   to avenge her son.
    At Heorot she arrived,   where the Ring-Danes

slept in the hall-space.　It was a sudden setback　　　　1280
for those dear-born earls　when Grendel's dam
passed through the gateway.　The panic was less
only by as much as　a maid's onslaught,
woman's war-rush is　from that of a well-armed man
when the iron-wound weapon,　wrought on the anvil –　　1285
the blood-stained sword　with its braided edge –
cuts the boar-crests　of an oncoming enemy.
The hard blade was　drawn in Heorot.
Above the seats were swords;　many a swart-rimmed shield
was hefted aloft.　When horror found them　　　　1290
there was no time for mail　or metal helmet.
Once she'd been spotted there　she wanted flight,
to save her own skin,　to escape, to flee...
But as she fled fenwards　her fingers found
one doomed fighter,　and held him fast.　　　　1295
He was of all hall-men　dearest to Hrothgar –
between the sundering seas,　in his serried forces,
a well-favoured　warrior, shield-fighter –
and was torn from bed.　(Beowulf himself
slept apart, in　a place granted　　　　1300
to the glorious Geat　after the treasure-giving.)
Shouting shook Heorot,　from the shadows she dragged
that gore-glazed claw,　and griefs as of old
returned in darkness.　It was a dear bargain:
on both sides they　were bound to pay　　　　1305
with their loved ones' lives,　and the lustrous king,
Hrothgar the Wise,　hoar-braided chief,
was soul-darkened　after he'd seen himself
that his dearest man　lay dead, lifeless.

　　Soon Beowulf was fetched,　famed, belated,　　　1310
to the battle-chamber.　In that bleak day-break
he went himself –　a sure champion –
with a handful of earls　to where Hrothgar sat:

after the woe-spell   would the All-Wielder
ever bring about   a change for the better?   1315
Battle's great champion   with his chosen men
crossed the hall-floor   (the hall-wood dinned)
and addressed Hrothgar,   Ingwin Hearth-Lord,
with candid words: had the king rested?
Such a needy summons   had surprised the night.   1320
    Hrothgar then spoke,   Helm of the Scyldings:
'Say nothing of rest.   Sorrow's come again
'to the Dane-people.   Death's taken Aeschere,
'the older brother   of Yrmenlaf
'and my rune-teller,   ready counsellor   1325
'and comrade in arms   in the clash of battle-lines.
'We defended ourselves   against foot-soldiers,
'boar-crests flaring... Such a best of brothers
'should any clansman   be, as Aeschere was.
'Some carrion-spirit   clutched and killed him   1330
'here, in Heorot.   How or where she
'went afterwards,   woman-shaped, in her
'new-bloated blood-feast,   no-one here knows.
'She paid the feud   you forced last night
'with Grendel, when your grip   gouged and tore him   1335
'because he'd thinned and killed   my fine clan-ranks
'for far too long.   He fell in battle,
'he forfeited life.   Yet now this fierce man-killer,
'another cruel ravager,   has come vengeful.
'Far has she carried   her feuding – or so   1340
'must many of my thanes   be thinking as they mourn
'their treasure-giver   in grief's mind-depths,
'appalled, heavy-hearted.   And powerless now the hand
'that once could grant   almost every desire.
    'Wise counsellors   have witnessed, they said –   1345
'sage ones among my people – have seen, they said,
'or glimpsed two such   terrible spirits,

'massive shape-haunters   on the moors' fastness,
'wan, murk-shrouded.   And one of the two,
'so far as their best   of their findings went,   1350
'had a woman's likeness.   Lack-formed, the other
'trailed wretchedly   down exile's tracks,
'man-shaped – but more   monster than man-like.
'"Grendel," they called him,   this yesterday's guest,
'in former days.   They knew of no father.   1355
'How time whelped them,   and from what turmoil,
'no-one could tell.   Now they live in the mist-lands,
'wolf-haunted slopes,   wind-stricken cliffs,
'on fierce fen-tracks   where water falls
'darkly down from   dreary rock-faces   1360
'and flows underground.   It's not far from here,
'as miles are reckoned,   that their mere stretches,
'overhung with   ice-covered trees,
'their roots fast in   rime and shadow.
'And there each midnight   a miracle can be seen –   1365
'flame on water.   The wisest that lives
'of this people's sons   hasn't plumbed those depths.
'Even the hunted hart,   the heath-chaser,
'strong-horned, fleeing   to the forest's edge
'when the dogs hound him   from the distance,   1370
'will baulk on the shore   and die on the bank
'before he'll swim his head.   It's a hideous place:
'storm-driven waterspouts   strike up darkly,
'rear at cloudscapes   when the roaring wind
'stirs sky to storm,   until the stricken air   1375
'of heaven itself must weep... Yet again our help
'must come from you alone.   That land you don't yet know,
'fatefullest of places,   nor whether you'll find there
'that much-glutted sinner.   Seek, then, if you dare it.
'This fight I'll repay   most properly,   1380
'with age-old treasure,   as I did earlier –

69

'with time-wrought gold –   if you return safely.'
    And Ecgtheow's son,   Beowulf, then said:
'Wise one, don't waste   your witness. It's better,
'always, to affirm   friendship by vengeance   1385
'than by endless grief.   All of us will perish –
'wait, sure to end.   Yet some before death
'may gain glory: great names survive
'longest, although   lifeless the fighter.
'So stand, lord: we   should look quickly   1390
'for the spoor, the tracks   of whoever spawned Grendel.
'And I promise you this: there's no place – no thicket,
'no weft of earth,   no wooded hillside
'nor rucked mere-bed   she'll rest, whatever her wishes.
'Today endure   with dire patience   1395
'each press of woe –   as I expect you shall.'
    The old man stood   astonished, gave thanks
to the mighty Lord   for such manly words.
Then for Hrothgar was prepared   a plume-maned horse.
It was saddled, bridled.   The sage chieftain   1400
rode in full tack while   the foot-soldiers
marched, shield-burdened.   Marks and foot-traces
were easily seen   on old bridleways.
They were tracks that ran   directly towards
murk-stained moorland   where the maimed hall-thane –   1405
best of those who   rebutted the attack
on Hrothgar's home –   had been hauled, lifeless.
The nobly born   battle-man then crossed
sheer stone-faces,   steepening pathways,
single-tracked trails   ending in terror   1410
on high headlands,   homes of water-snakes.
With a few clever   kinsmen he forged
ahead, to scout,   scope out the place,
until suddenly   he saw the trees
leaning lifelessly   over a litter of stone: 1415

the stricken wood.   Water lapped there,
turbid and bloodied.   To the Scylding troop,
to each Dane present,   it was a perilous grief
to endure – fiercely   frightening to many –
when on that high cliff-fall   they came across   1420
the awful thing   that was Aeschere's head.
   The troop looked on   a lake – blood-mired,
boiling with heart's-gore.   A horn gave out
stammering fate-song.   Foot-soldiers sat,
glimpsed things writhing   in the thick water,   1425
squirming sea-dragons   scouring wave-depths
like those harmful beasts   lurking among headlands,
which at dark daybreak   often deem it fit –
they're worms, snake-coils –   to wreak havoc,
disaster to ships   on short sail-roads.   1430
Startled, those serpents   like stones sank away,
submerged, enraged   by the ringing horn-note.
One Geat loosed off   an arrow from afar
at a swimming creature,   a swift war-dart,
from Beowulf's position.   The beast was slow,   1435
painfully hindered,   and perished swimming.
Then barbed boar-spears   brutally, quickly
worked at waves'-edge,   wound-opening malice,
drew onto the headland   their dangerous guest,
strange wave-crosser: an astonishing corpse   1440
under the eyes of men.
                    Meanwhile Beowulf
clad himself in armour,   careless of danger.
That war-corselet,   woven cunningly,
had pledged duty   to explore the mere.
It knew how to keep   breath's cave unharmed;   1445
neither fierce attack   nor foe's grasping
malice ever could harm   the man wearing it.
And the helm's glister   protected his head –

which would merge with   the mere's soundings,
turn through water's-moil,   a treasured object,   1450
encircled, endowed.   In days long ago
a smith worked it   with wondrous skill,
armed it with boar-brass,   so that afterwards
no sword, no battle-mace   could bite through it.
And not the least aid to   his legendary strength   1455
was the blade lent by   Hrothgar's bondsman:
that miraculous hilt   was called Hrunting,
was hugely the best   of inherited treasures –
sharp, iron-edged;   shining, venom-carved,
hardened in war's-blood.   It had never weakened yet   1460
in anyone's grip   if they understood its use
and dared undergo   danger, battle-journeys
to enemy dwellings.   Due was its moment:
again it would practise   its gift of valour.

    Hrothgar's kinsman   didn't care to recall,   1465
in his cunning power,   his putrid words –
besotted, wine-glutted –   when his weapon was given
to the better swordsman.   His baleful self
wouldn't risk its life   under the roiling waves.
He lost courage,   therefore lost respect,   1470
the possibility of fame.   With Beowulf it was otherwise
after he'd prepared for   the press of the fray.

    Beowulf, Ecgtheow's child,   chose then to speak:
'Consider, beloved   leader of Healfdanes –
their guide, counsel,   gold-protector –   1475
in this time's readiness,   what we two agreed:
if in your service   I should ever be
parted from those living,   then you'd be pleased to take
after that fatality   a father's place.
Be you protector   to my troop of thanes,   1480
close kinsmen, if   combat claim me,
and – beloved Hrothgar –   to Hygelac send

those gifts of treasure you've graced me with.
Then will the Geatish lord, loved son of Hrethel,   1485
be able to see, discern in the gifting,
how a great ring-giver, glorious in virtue,
granted me bounty. And... Bold Unferth:
this wrought way-sword your reputation
gave me, havoc-edged. With Hrunting I   1490
shall endure judgement, be juried by death.'
Those words spoken, the Weders' chief
strode off, away, not waiting for reply.
The waters' whelm, wave-chaos, enwrapped
a mortal swimmer. It was most of that day   1495
before he could fathom, find lake-bottom.
    Hundreds of half-years she'd held, guarded
the flood's expanse, fiercely ravenous,
greedy, terrible. She could tell at once
that one of human kind swam through her holt.   1500
She grappled him, grabbed at the garb of war
with hideous claws, hauled at him as they plummeted,
but couldn't do harm. His corselet, spell-woven,
couldn't be penetrated; her probing nails
found no purchase on the patterned chain-locks.   1505
But in their plummeting fall her claws fastened
on the corselet's cover. She carried him to her lair.
No matter how brave, Beowulf could not
wield his weapons there: worm-writhing devils,
enraged sea-monsters, rucked around him,   1510
their sword-like tusks snagging at his armour,
teeth tearing him. In the turmoil he saw
something impossible, some sort of hell,
which no water could overwhelm or reach.
A vaulted roof kept the rushing lake-flood   1515
from falling, and fire flickered there within,
its pale flame-tongues faint and putrid.

The good warrior;   the witch of mud,
mere's brutality.   Finding his battle-axe
at last he struck,   no restraint in the swing: 1520
around her head   ring-patterns sang out
their stricken war-song.   But the stranger found
the battle-knife's edge   had no easy bite,
could injure nothing: edge failed its man
in his second of need.   Then he suffered the hours: 1525
hand-to-hand combat,   his helmet split,
fate-struck chain-mail... For the first time his
dear-made war-trappings   left their doom doubtful.
    Still, resolute was   that stern-minded
kinsman of Hygelac,   and careful of fame.   1530
He cast off his sword,   with its serpentine patterns.
Anger left it.   It lay on the ground,
strong and steel-edged.   But it was his own strength he'd trust –
that mighty grip.   So men must do
if they think to gain   in the thresh of war   1535
long-lasting fame,   nor life over-reckon.
    Then the Geat warrior   seized Grendel's mother
by the shoulders, sure   in that unsure combat.
He flung her about,   battle-boldened.
She landed in dirt,   livid foe-woman –   1540
quickly quit him –   requited the blow –
claws grabbed at him –   crushed him breathless.
Even that mightiest of men,   almost overmastered,
stricken half to death,   stumbled wearily.
Deadly, visitant,   she drew her knife,   1545
the swart-edged blade.   For her son, vengeance –
for her only kin... But on his chest's axle
lay the supple chain-mail.   It saved his life,
withstood the ravages   of ripping knife-point.
There might Ecgtheow's son   early have perished,   1550
in that submerged country – he was the might of Geats –

had not the wrought war-shirt   worked its magic,
spell-bound battle-net;   had not the spirit of God,
all-knowing in   the numbers of war,
the heavens' Reasoner,   rightly and easily   1555
deemed for Beowulf... who dragged himself to his feet.
    Among the den's debris   one sword endured,
age-old giant-work   whose edge hadn't aged,
whose memory was honour: a meritable weapon,
but so heavy with merit   that no other man   1560
could ever have used   its ancient weight
and purpose there   in the play of battle.
Yet Hrothgar's man,   unhesitating,
seized the wrapped war-hilt –   in wanhope struck,
despairing, with the patterned   sprig of war-steel.   1565
It buried brutally   in her body; her neck
cracked; cartilage   from her spine's column
spilled from the spear-point.   She sprawled to the ground;
moisture stained the edge;   man exulted.
    Surrounded by light,   riddled with brightness   1570
like the holy, clear,   heavenly shining
that's the sky's candle,   he squinted at the cave,
hugged the wall's-edge,   Hygelac's champion,
hefted again his   hard-hilted weapon,
his mind busy   with anger. That blade   1575
was still useful,   since his stern intent
was to repay Grendel   for those appalling visits
he'd made to the Danes,   no more than for the time
when he'd torn Hrothgar's   hearth-friends from dreams,
ripped them from sleeping,   swallowed alive   1580
fifteen fighting-men   from the Danes' family.
And there were others, countless,   whom he'd carried off
to his loathsome dam,   to their lake's squalor.
That cruel ravager   was quit in full
for his vicious crimes: his victor saw   1585

75

the mangled remains –   Grendel, mortal –
among death's litter.   Their downfall had caused
carnage in Heorot.   He hacked at the corpse.
Two deaths it suffered   in that terrible blow –
its body hewn, and   its head carved off.   1590
    Watchers with Hrothgar,   who waited on the bank
and gazed at the lake's   glaze, now looked at
dead blooms of blood   drifting in the currents,
a gathering stain.   Grey-chinned elders
murmured together   about Beowulf's merits...   1595
didn't expect to see   such a prince again...
wouldn't ever return   triumphant, back
to our most royal...   Many there alleged
that the pool's she-wolf   had pulled him apart.
Noon came and went.   At the ness, Hrothgar's   1600
troop began to   return homewards.
Those heroes dispersed,   while the horror-stricken
Geats continued   to gaze at the mere.
They wished without hope   to witness their beloved
emerge, and in the flesh...
                    In a moment,   1605
as if an icicle burnt,   Beowulf's battle-sword
began to waste away.   A wonder, certainly:
it vanished altogether,   like ice ungirded
by the Father of heaven   from frost-fetters
when He who sways   the seasons and their times,   1610
Wielder of World-truth,   unbinds water.
Yet the Geats' leader,   gathering booty,
seeing loot and treasure   left around him,
took only the monster's head   and the maimed sword-hilt –
a stained bounty.   (Burnt and melted   1615
was the sword's broad blade.   The blood of the one
killed in his den was   death's corrosion.)
    Then he was swimming,   searching, diving

upwards, still living   beyond the last of strife.
Cleansed, purified   was that expanse of lake   1620
and its ribbed shoreline,   reft of the ghost-shuck
whose life had been finished   among the frets of time.
    He swam to the land,   Helm of seafarers,
with determined strokes,   untiring, exultant
at the heavy plunder   he had with him.   1625
Towards him they moved,   remembering their thanks –
great-hearted thanes –   to God, who had delivered
their chief unharmed,   whole to their watching.
They soon stripped from   their strong chieftain
helmet and byrnie.   The huge whelming   1630
of water calmed   under blood-coloured clouds.
Then forth they went   over the foot-trails,
their hearts alight;   they hurried over the paths,
known bridleways.   They were bold as kings.
Cumbrously from the cliff-top   they carried the head,   1635
and with great difficulty,   yet each was glad,
determined not to fail.   It took four to carry
the heavy burden   that was Grendel's head
back to the gold-hall   on a gore-streaked stake,
until they came at last   to the counsel-hall: 1640
fourteen fight-hardened   and fierce soldiers
of the Geatish troop   and their glorious chief,
a proud press on   the surrounding plain.
In battle-order   Beowulf went in –
lord-like and happy,   lit by honour,   1645
by doom-getting –   to greet Hrothgar.
Then onto the hall-floor   they hauled the head
of Grendel by the hair,   into the great mead-space.
To drinkers there, to the queen   it was a dreadful sight,
wondrous and horrible.   They witnessed it in awe.   1650
    Beowulf, Ecgtheow's   offspring, then spoke:
'So. What you see here,   son of Healfdan,

'Merit of Scyldings,   is the mere's legacy,
'brought to you gladly   as a battle-token.
'I barely survived   that viciousness alive,   1655
'that underwater war,   and the work only dared
'with difficulty.   Doubtful it was:
'the fight would have finished   without the Father's aid.
'From Hrunting I had   no help in the struggle:
'keen though the blade is,   it accomplished nothing.   1660
'Yet I was granted   by the God of men
'sight of a wonder –   a sword hanging
'from the wall, age-worked.   (So, often He guides
'those utterly alone.)   I drew that ancient weapon,
'and when time favoured it,   in the turmoil slew   1665
'those nest-keepers.   The narrow-curled blade,
'wave-patterned, melted: it welled with blood,
'hottest battle-sweat.   Its hilt I pulled –
'– plundered – from my enemies,   and paid for their crimes
'among the death-ravaged Danes.   That due was right.   1670
'Here I promise you: that Heorot's granted peace,
'so that you'll sleep sorrowless,   safe among your kinsmen.
'Neither for your nation,   nor your bondsmen
'canny or youthful,   will you be claimed by dread,
'leader of Scyldings,   when you think of life   1675
'or death among your earls –   as you did before.'
     Then the golden hilt   was given to the hands
of the ancient seer,   the old warlord.
Wrought once by giants,   after the wicked were doomed
that legacy passed   to the lord of the Danes,   1680
wondrous smith-work. And so the world spewed out
the grim-hearted,   God's adversary,
murderous, guilty – and his mother too.
The sword-hilt passed   to the sovereign best
of those who dealt in treasures   in Danish lands –   1685
no better in the world   between the bounded seas.

Hrothgar then spoke.   He inspected the hilt,
ancient heirloom   etched with its origins:
of the first fighting,   when the flood carried off
in its clabbering whelm   all kin of giants.   1690
They suffered badly –   a race sundered
from the eternal Lord;   their last reward
was granted by God   in a glut of flood.

On the sword-hilt's skein,   on the sweltered gold,
also ran, clear-marked   in rune-carved letters,   1695
an inscription that told   who'd first turned the sword,
the cherished iron,   choicest of blades –
dragon-etched, wave-hilted.   Then the wise one spoke,
Healfdan's great son.   They fell silent.
'It can truly be said   by he who truth and right   1700
'embodies in this clan,   who recalls all of old,
'chosen Dane ward,   that this chief was born
'the greater man!   Your glory is and shall spread,
'my dear Beowulf,   to distant lands –
'yours, over what people so ever.   With complete patience you
                                                           guard it,   1705
'combining strength with wisdom.   Still now and always, my
                                                           friendship
'I affirm, as we agreed before.   And you must be a firm comfort,
'and a long-lasting one,   a leader, to your tribe,
'to its heroes a help.
                      Heremod was not so
'for Ecgwela's sons,   the Scyldings of old.   1710
'He didn't grow to joy,   but to great slaughter,
'death and destruction   of the Danish tribe.
'His closest friends   he killed while they ate.
'He was enraged, brooding.   At last he bent alone,
'that once-famous figure,   from the fair world's joys,   1715
'although Almighty God   in merit and power
'had advanced him far –   further in fact than

'all other men.   Yet in his mind there spawned
'some blood-hunger.   He blessed no Dane
'with due ring-giving.   Dream-darkened he   1720
'lived, lashed by spirit –   a lingering trouble
'to his tribe for years.   Be taught by that:
'understand true goodness!   This tale I tell
'wintered in wisdom.
                                A wonder to relate,
'how mighty God   to all man-kind   1725
'in His large knowing   allots wisdom,
'land and title;   He controls everything.
'In His love, sometimes   He lets the thoughts
'of well-kinned man   wander widely,
'in his home hands him   the happiness to rule   1730
'no strange territory,   but the stronghold of men;
'makes parts of the world –   a wide kingdom –
'subject to him,   so that his very self can't
'imagine in its folly   how it will ever finish.
'In abundant bliss   he's borne, never stopped   1735
'by illness or age,   nor by inner malice
'ever soul-darkened,   nor by any enmity
'showing sharp hatred... The whole of his world
'is wound to his will.   The worse he's never known –
'until somewhere within,   while his soul's keeper   1740
'and guardian sleeps,   some unguarded pride
'flourishes, increases.   He's fast-set in that sleep,
'too bound with cares;   his killer's too close,
'with foul bow-instincts   and with fleet arrows.
'Then he's heart-stricken   under his helmet   1745
'by the bitter needle –   he knows no defence –
'and the crazed beckonings   of his accursed spirit.
'Too little it now seems,   what he ruled so long.
'Cruel and covetous   turns his craving mind,
'whose pride gives no gold.   He forgets or ignores   1750

'the good future   God gave him once,
'the great Shielder's   share of honour.
'And so in the end   it also must happen
'that leased life-home,   the flesh, decays,
'is doomed, perishes;   another prince succeeds,   1755
'one who guiltlessly   gives out treasures,
'fair, ancient wealth,   and fears no terrors.
'Guard against such hate-lashing,   honoured Beowulf
'and best of men.   Choose the better road – to
'eternal gains.   Give pride no place,   1760
'my beloved champion.   It shall linger a while,
'the glory of your power,   but presently it shall be
'that sickness or the sword   shall unseat your strength,
'or the flames' embrace,   or the flood's whelming,
'or the blade in spite,   or the spear in flight,   1765
'or the horror of age,   or the once-keen eyes
'failing, dim-shadowed;   and soon it shall be due
'to you, dear warrior: death shall overpower you.
    'And so I've ruled Ring-Danes   under the roiling clouds
'half a century;   saved, sheltered them   1770
'when many tribes warred   here on middle-earth
'with ash and edge,   until any enemy
'was under heaven, for me,   of no heavy account.
'Yet... A change happened,   here in this homeland.
'Grief rushed from joy   after Grendel's coming –   1775
'an ancient foe: adversary and intruder.
'His dire visits   I endured, always
'bleakly and in sorrow.   May blessings be to God,
'the eternal Lord,   that I've lived this long,
'could see with my own eyes,   after such long struggle,   1780
'that battle-scarred   and blood-stained head!
'Go now to the benches,   join the blessed feasting
'in your gallant honour.   A great many
'treasures shall be shared when   it's turned morning.'

The Geat was gladdened,   gained the trestles   1785
quickly, as the Wise one   kindly commanded.
It was as of old   for that ancient race
of brave ones: anew   for those bench-sitters
a feast was laid.   Lingering night-helm
shadowed the carousers.   Then the veteran ranks   1790
stood up: grey-haired   Hrothgar, age-stricken
Hrothgar, sought bed.   Beowulf also –
brave shield-bearer – would surely seek rest.
At once an attendant thane   thought to guide him,
that weary traveller   of the wide distances.   1795
(In those far-off days   a fighter's needs,
such as any soldier   or sailor would have,
were all cared for   out of courtesy.)
   His great heart rested;   the hall climbed sky,
gold-worked, vaulted;   guests slept sound there   1800
until the pale raven   in unresting joy
witnessed day's-breaking.   There was bright scurrying...
            ...   Warriors got busy –
hearts of the high-born   thought of home, and kin,
and would fare homewards,   and far from that place   1805
the visitor, in glee,   looked to regain his vessel.
Beowulf ordered then   that Ecglaf's son
be brought Hrunting,   and bade him receive
the cost-wrought blade.   Brief thanks he added
for the loan, saying   the sword was good,   1810
mighty in warfare;   such a weapon's edge
could bear no blame: that was bold, generous.
By then the warriors   in their wrought armour
were eager to leave.   The one honoured
by the Danes approached   the place and throne   1815
where Hrothgar sat   and hailed him like a prince.
   Beowulf, Ecgtheow's   offspring, then spoke:
'And now we want to say –   as sailors, come

'from a far country –   that we feel it's time
'to seek Hygelac.   Here all we wished   1820
'was done for our desires: you dealt with us well.
'If there ever on earth   was anything I could do
'to merit more   of your mind's honour,
'dear lord of men,   than I've done thus far
'by prowess in arms,   then I'll soon prove ready.   1825
'If I should find out   across the flood's expanse
'that neighbouring tribes   should attempt terror,
'as your enemies did   in the old times, then
'I'll bring a thousand   thanes to help you,
'hand-picked fighters.   Of Hygelac I know,   1830
'though the Geat king   may yet be young
'to rule a tribe,   that he'd be an untiring
'support in both deeds   and words, so that I could show due
'honour to you, bring you   an ash-spear forest,
'bring aid and strength,   if ever you were in need.   1835
'And whenever Hrethric,   that noble son,
'decides to come   to the court of the Geats,
'there he'll find friendship: far lands are better
'sought by people   powerful themselves.'
Hrothgar then spoke,   handed back an answer: 1840
'It's a witting God   that gave these words
'and sayings to your heart.   I've never yet heard
'a wiser speech   by one so young.
'You're strong in power,   steeped in wisdom,
'canny thought-wielder!   It's likely, I think,   1845
'if it should come to pass   that the keen spear-point,
'if sword-grim battle,   take Hrethel's son,
'stricken age or iron   destroy your king,
'that youthful lord,   and if you are yet living,
'that the clan of Geats   could have no better   1850
'in coming to choose   a king over others,
'a ward for its hoard,   should you wish to rule

83

'your kinsman's clan. Your qualities I like the better,
'beloved Beowulf, the longer they're known.
'What you've determined is that two peoples –   1855
'the Geatish tribe, the Spear-Danes' troops –
'should share the peace, shed thoughts of war,
'the dire hatreds they endured before.
'To come, while I rule this wide kingdom,
'shall be a common wealth: we'll greet one another   1860
'out of goodness over the gannet's bath.
'Each ship, ring-prowed, over our riven sea
'shall bring tokens, treasures. I know these two peoples,
'as firm as friends as they were as foes,
'shall be ever blameless, in the ancient manner.'   1865
And then to the Geat that great chieftain
of the Danish tribe gave twelve treasures
and urged him to return homewards with such tokens,
seek out his kin quickly and safely.
King and warrior then kissed and embraced,   1870
Scylding battle-lord and best of thanes,
a twin neck-grasp. Tears fell from Hrothgar,
from the greying whiskers. He was in the grip of thoughts
both old and wise – wise were strongest –
and imagined they'd meet many times more in   1875
duty and council. So dear to him was Beowulf
that he couldn't restrain his strong tear-whelm,
and a remote sadness within his mind-bounds
firm-heartedly formed on such a dear one
and burnt in blood. Beowulf meanwhile   1880
walked the grass-mound proudly, gold-armoured,
triumphal in treasure. The tall ship rode
anchor, waiting for its owner and lord.
On their homeward crossing Hrothgar's generosity
was often praised. They said that was one king   1885
utterly blameless – until age took away

due joys of strength,   as it does to so many.
   They came to the tide   tearing in spirit,
those young warriors,   wearing ring-mail,
close-locked battle-shirts.   The coastguard spotted   1890
the heroes' return.   Time turned again:
no insult now   from the neb of cliffs,
no rearing alarm.   He rode towards them,
said how welcome they'd be   to the Weder people,
ship-borne soldiers   in their shining trappings.   1895
On the sand rested   the ring-prowed vessel,
a broad-based keel   ballasted with war-gear,
with horses and treasure,   its mast towering
over Hrothgar's presents,   his hoard of wealth.
   To the coast-guard   a costly sword   1900
was given, gold-chased: such a fabled gift
afterwards made him   a worthier man
on the mead-benches.   And Beowulf left,
furrowed deep water   on his way homeward.
Sheets sang on mast;   the shrouds of the sea   1905
fastened filled sails;   the foam-traveller,
the wave-dancer,   by wind unchecked,
was unhindered.   Onwards it fared,
froth-necked, floating   further over wave-ruck,
its prow cleaving   the currents of the sea,   1910
until they could make out   the cliffs of home,
Geatish headlands.   The keel grounded,
weather-stricken, rested   on well-known land.
   Quick to the tide's-edge   was the coast's watchman,
who'd scanned the current   eagerly for their coming –   1915
a long lookout   for beloved comrades.
To the beach he moored   the broad-set hull;
anchored it with rope-bands   lest the rip and power
of the waves would catch   the costly timbers;
ordered Beowulf's   beautiful treasures   1920

to be brought ashore.   It was only a short distance
to where they could seek   the source of treasure,
Hygelac Hrethling,   whose home he shared
with his warrior troop   at the tide's boundary.
Splendid, that stronghold;   spirited, its chieftain,   1925
at home in his hall;   and Hygd, his queen,
though young, was mannered   with much wisdom
despite the few winters   she'd witnessed at court.
She was Haereth's daughter,   and duly gave out –
no niggardliness – unnumbered gifts   1930
for Geatish merits.   She was no Modthryth,
a torment to her clan,   who did terrible crimes:
none – no tribesman,   no retainer,
none except her husband – none ever dared
while day lasted   to look into her eyes.   1935
If so, he could count   on cruelty: shackles,
blood-slicked slaughter-bonds;   soon afterwards
the sword's shearing,   the descending cut
of the doom-worked blade: the death sentence
would be carried out.   That's no queen's custom   1940
or woman's practice,   however peerless she is.
She should weave peace, a queen,   not require the life
of innocent men   for imagined insults.
Still, Hemming's man   put a stop to her –
and drinkers once told   a different tale,   1945
of how she was less spiteful,   less of a torment,
less malice-eaten,   after she was married, given
in her gold-worked dress   to the great Offa,
then a young fighter,   fierce and valued:
she'd been led, taken   by a loving father   1950
over the tawny seas.   So, afterwards,
she graced the throne,   was greatly famed
for her continuing   kind practices,
for the love she bore   her lord, the best

of mankind's heroes   (so I heard it said),   1955
the very finest   of that far-flung race,
sea-scattered man.   And so Offa –
spear-keen in war,   and widely honoured
for his mind and gifts –   with wisdom and merit
ruled his kingdom.   His kin and son   1960
was Eomer, Hemming's   help in battle,
Garmund's grand-nephew: he was good at war.
   Battle-hard Beowulf   and his band of men
stepped on the sand-strip   at the sea's edges,
on the wide-curved strand.   The world's candle   1965
shone with south-light.   Their sea-crossing
they'd survived. They crossed   keenly to where Hygelac –
bane of Ongentheow –   sat in his burg-hall,
a young princeling   reputed for goodness
and ring-sharing.   To royal Hygelac   1970
the news was brought   of Beowulf's coming:
the clan's captain   was in the enclosed forecourt –
solid shield-bearer...   is safe and sound...
is hale and well... is on his way...returned.
Space was quickly made   at the king's command   1975
for such famed visitors.   And in they filed.
   Prince, survivor;   loyal survivor,
prince: the kinsmen sat,   after the kind customs
and ceremonial words   had met Beowulf,
his men and their merits.   Mead-flagons were passed.   1980
Haereth's daughter,   in duty and love
for her people, bore   the best of vessels
to the heroes' hands.   Hygelac began
courteously to question   his kinsman, there
in the towering hall.   His curiosity teemed   1985
as to what the Sea-Geats   had seen on their adventures.
   'Beowulf, fame-honoured,   what befell you
'after you suddenly   decided to travel

'salt-laden seas   and seek combat,
'strife in Heorot?   And did Hrothgar –   1990
'that great war-chief –   and his well-known woes
'have any remedy?   I was anxious:
'many sorrows seethed.   You're so valued
'I didn't trust your going.   Often I told you
'not to think of that wraith,   rumoured carnage,   1995
'but let the South-Danes   themselves settle
'Grendel's challenge.   Yet to God be thanks
'you're sound, granted   a safe return.'
    Beowulf, Ecgtheow's   offspring, then spoke:
'It's no deep secret,   dear lord Hygelac: 2000
'many a man knows now   of the mighty fight,
'the great contest,   between Grendel and me,
'in that perilous place   where for so many people
'of the warlike Danes   he'd caused so much damage,
'lifelong viciousness.   I avenged it all: 2005
'no Grendel-kin   would ever be keen to boast
'of that dire dawn-clash   to any earth-dweller,
'no matter how long   the last of those devils
'might linger in malice.'
                 'On landing I came
'to the Hall of Rings   to greet Hrothgar.   2010
'As soon as he knew   my mind's nature,
'that great kinsman   of great Healfdan,
'he urged me to sit   among his own offspring.
'Joyous, that gathering: in the jostle of life
'under heaven's vaulting   I've heard of no better   2015
'sounding hall-banter.   Sometimes the queen –
'famed peace-pledger –   passed between the benches,
'gracing the younger,   gifting a token
'to the seasoned,   before she sat again.
'And in sweet duty   Hrothgar's daughter   2020
'also bore the wrought ale-cup   through the ranks of men.

'As she passed the studded   and precious vessel
'to warriors nearby,   from neighbours I heard
'she was named Freawaru.   Fresh, gold-dowried,
'to the princely son   of Froda she's promised.   2025
'The Scylding lord   and people's shepherd
'arranged the alliance,   reckoned carefully
'that with such a woman   he could settle a part
'of former feuds.   Yet after a leader's fall
'it's rare for the spear   to rest anywhere,   2030
'to blunt or bend,   whatever the bride's value.'
    'Think how the leader,   lord of Heathobards,
'would feel as they went   to such a woman's wedding,
'entertained there   as attendants of Danes.
'On the Danes glitter   dear-bought heirlooms,   2035
'hardened, ring-locked –   Heathobard treasures,
'worn in battle   as long as battle lasted,
'until they'd witnessed   warriors' destruction,
'the lives of friends   lost in shield-shatter,
'beloved companions   led into slaughter.   2040
'And then at the beer-pledging,   suppose an old,
'ash-bent veteran   eyes such an heirloom,
'death's memento.   Memory burns him.
'Darkened in spirit,   he addresses a young
'warrior, tempts him,   wakes in his mind-mood   2045
'renewed war-wrath   by speaking these words:
' "Can you see, young one,   that time-worked sword?
' "It was your father's.   When he went to fight
' "under his grim battle-mask   on that brutal last
' "campaign he carried   that precious blade.   2050
' "War-Danes slew him.   After Withergild lay dead
' "among his fallen men   the foul Scyldings
' "claimed the slaughter-place.   And now some son
' "of those same killers   in the same stolen
' "war-gear struts round   under our rafters,   2055

' "mouthing off in armour   that you own by right." '
'With such turbulent words   it's trouble his memories
'stir up, until   a time shall come
'when the fierce bill-bite   takes Freawaru's thane.
'He's brought from life   blood-freaked, and sleeps   2060
'because of his father's deeds.   And duly his killer
'escapes alive: he knows his country well.
'And then...? Both parties   are bound to break
'the old blood-oaths;   in Ingeld shall teem
'fatal enmity,   while his former lust   2065
'for the woman shall cool   in his killing griefs.
'And so I don't consider   the sworn friendship
'of the Heathobard tribe   for Danes trustworthy,
'or their talk of peace.

                  Now to return to telling
'something of Grendel,   so that you'll gain knowledge,   2070
'lord and hoard-sharer,   of what happened next
'in the fierce hand-rush.   When heaven's gem
'had slid below ground   this...guest...came on,
'vile and angry,   visitor in darkness,
'where we – as yet unharmed –   guarded Heorot.   2075
'Hondscio was first   to fall in that battle,
'was first to be doomed.   He was furthest away,
'a gallant fighter,   well-girded with weapons.
'And Grendel became   his corpse-maker:
'that beloved comrade   was eaten alive.   2080
'Nor yet did Grendel want –   greedy, blood-toothed,
'goaded to slaughter –   to go from the hall
'empty-handed.   In his unhallowed strength
'he made trial of me,   tested my courage
'in his powerful grip.   A pouch of sorts   2085
'hung there wide-necked,   worked from strangeness,
'intricately decorated,   with a devious clasp –
'wrought with devil-craft   and with dragons' skins.

'I was sinless, yet   it was there inside
'that this malice-worker   wanted to stuff me   2090
'as one of many.   But it wasn't to be:
'stiffened with anger   I stood upright.
'It's too long to tell   how I gave return
'to that tribe-scather   for each teeming wrong,
'how I honoured you, lord,   and our own people   2095
'in works and deeds.   A while afterwards
'he lived, escaped   on his way, lingering,
'yet he'd left something   of himself in Heorot:
'his torn-off hand.   It was in terror he left.
'He sank into the depths   of the dismal mere.   2100
    'The Scylding lord   paid me lavishly
'for that bloodied meeting   in bountiful gold,
'dear-kept treasures.   When dawn broke again,
'when we'd sat again   to a glorious feast,
'harp-song told tales: Hrothgar himself   2105
'related stories,   relived from the past.
'Sometimes for pleasure   he played the harp,
'song-strung game-wood;   sometimes he told
'of the tragic and true,   or twisted things
'were retold rightly   from his roomy heart;   2110
'and sometimes, too,   knowing time's passing,
'that old veteran   would vividly tell
'of youth, battle-strength,   of his yesterdays.
'He had overwintered much   and gained wisdom.
    'A whole day long   we lingered inside,   2115
'relishing our pleasures,   until ragged nightfall
'brought dark again.   And duly she –
'Grendel's mother –   gained soon afterwards
'revenge for the death   of her vicious son,
'the Weders' war-hate.   She walked from sorrow   2120
'to take vengeance.   Vicious as her offspring,
'she was intent, evil: it was Aeschere,

'wise old counsellor,   who was claimed from life.
'Nor could the exhausted Danes,   in that damaged daybreak,
'cremate his corpse,   lie the mortal body   2125
'of that fine clansman   on the funeral pyre:
'she had carried him off   like a carcase,
'then mauled at him   beneath the mountain stream.
'It broke Hrothgar,   this bitterest of griefs,
'most terrible of all   that time had dealt.   2130
'He asked, stricken –   he urged in your name –
'that in the waters' thrashing,   the waves tumult,
'I should show gallantry,   or find glory,
'should wager life.   Rewards were promised.
'It's now well known that   in the waters' whelm   2135
'I found the depths guarded   by the grimmest of spirits.
'It was hand-to-hand,   our fierce hatred.
'Blood stained the waves.   With a blade-keen sword
'I carved at her head,   cut Grendel's dam
'deep underground in   her ghoulish cavern.   2140
'With difficulty, I survived   undoomed, was spared.
'Again Hrothgar,   Healfdan's offspring,
'gave many treasures   most royally.
'He was his people's king,   knew the proper customs.
'I'd lost nothing,   relinquished no strength;   2145
'he gifted me gold   from his great treasury,
'Healfdan's successor –   I had my pick.
'It's this that I wish,   my warrior prince –
'this graced legacy –   to give to you.
'Everything still finds   its favour in you;   2150
'and except for you, my king,   I have no kin.'
   Battle-steeped helmet,   boar-crest standard,
iron-ringed war-shirt,   etched, ancient blade:
he ordered them brought,   went on with his tale.
   'This war-keen gear   Hrothgar gave me,   2155
'wise and generous.   Some witness and words

'he said I should give   about such a great legacy.
'It was Heorogar –   king of the Scyldings,
'and brave Hrothgar's   older brother –
'who had it in long keeping.   Yet he'd never left it –   2160
'this high-piled treasure –   to his son, Heoroward,
'for all his merits.   May you use it well!'
   I heard that four horses   followed the treasure-gift –
apple-tawny, swift,   and all alike –
after the gear of war.   Gladly he gave them,   2165
crest, metal and steeds: so should any kinsman do,
not craft a mesh   out of malice for others,
or with secret arts   ensure the death
of close comrades.   Hygelac was kin;
faithful was his nephew   in the fiercest strife.   2170
Each was mindful   of the other's well-being.
   Beowulf, I heard,   offered Hygd the queen
the cost-worked jewel,   gem-studded necklace
which Wealhtheow gave,   and three war-horses,
supple, saddle-bright.   After she'd received these gifts   2175
the bright collar   adorned her breast.
   And so Beowulf,   Ecgtheow's fine son,
was known both for war   and for wise actions.
He lived rightly: never took the life
of a man while drunk   nor let malice drive him,   2180
but his mighty strength –   mankind's best gift,
ordained by God –   he guarded, for battle.
It had been otherwise.   He'd been a humbled youth.
The sons of the Geats   said he was a No-good.
On the mead-benches   Geat commanders   2185
gave him no honour.   He was of no account.
He was slow, they said –   slow or lazy.
('Too feeble,' said the chiefs.)   Yet a change happened
worth those miseries   for such a well-blessed man.
   King Hygelac,   clan's protector,   2190

ordered Hrethel's   heirloom fetched in,
a wonder of gold.   Among the Geats there'd been
no greater treasure   among time-worked swords.
It was this he laid   on Beowulf's lap,
granting him also   gift-stool and hall,   2195
seven thousand hides   of land. (They both held
by ancient right   of ownership
land in their country.   The loftier in rank
ruled the most and best   of that broad kingdom.)
    In later days,   after the lash of battle,   2200
after Hygelac's death   and Heardred's fall –
when swords turned slayers   under shield-swaying
and the blood-fretted,   feuding Scylfings
committed violence   in a most vicious time,
from envy attacking   Hereric's nephew –   2205
so it happened,   so came about
that the broad kingdom   passed to Beowulf.
More than properly   were his people ruled
fifty winters –   he was a wise ruler,
capable warden –   until a criminal One,   2210
a dragon, in doom's   dark began ruling.
A hoard he watched   from his high barrow,
steep place of stones.   His sty's entrance
lay under it, undiscovered...
An unknown man went inside...   2215
... with his hand...   from the heathen hoard...
... the age-wrought treasure   that he afterwards...
...though he was reft,   robbed while sleeping,
by a thief's cunning.   Then kin and land
and people discovered   the scale of his wrath.   2220
    The dragon's treasure   wasn't disturbed by force;
who woke the dragon   wasn't wilful or vicious.
Exiled, distressed,   he'd struggled away
from his people's malice,   men-blows, insult;

94

he was need's fugitive,   a fellow of guilt,   2225
stumbling on it...   Straightaway he
found that...for the visitant   violence lay waiting;
yet the wretched...   ...
...   ... created
...   danger to whoever ransacked   2230
the costly cup.   Incalculable, the amount
of ancient treasure   in that earth-barrow.
    Many years before,   a mortal, unknown,
had thoughtfully hidden   a huge inheritance –
dear-bought treasures of   time's noble race.   2235
Death destroyed them: death doomed all those
old yesterdays.   But one man, the last
man among clansmen,   who'd remained longest,
sorrowed as he guarded   those gathered treasures,
expecting he'd be allowed   to look on the hoard   2240
for only the briefest time.   He found a barrow prepared,
ready, unoccupied,   a rift by the sea –
in a high headland,   hard to access.
He bore inside   the baleful treasure,
that guardian of rings –   glittering plate, with gold
its worthiest part –   with words of farewell: 2245
'Now hold, O earth,   since heroes cannot,
'the inheritance of earls –   once, yes, obtained
'from you nobly.   But now battle-death,
'stricken disaster,   has destroyed each of
'those, my companions: they're perished, all those   2250
'who witnessed joy.   They woke from life,
'abandoned it. And now?   No one. Who'll brandish sword?
'Polish up the plating   on this patterned flagon,
'this glittering goblet?   Gone, all of them.
'The hardened helm,   hued with gold-work,   2255
'shall be lustre-deprived: those who prepared such
'bold battle-masks   have been borne away;

'and this coat of mail,   knowing in conflict
'the bite of iron,   bludgeon of shields,
'decays, posthumous;   nor shall these corselets follow   2260
'heroes, ring out   everywhere in train
'of war-leaders.   The winsome harp;
'music's intricacy;   the mettled hawk
'flying through the hall;   or horse, eagerly
'tramping the courtyard.   Their triumph is death,   2265
'that has dismissed so many   of mortal kind.'
   Grief piled on grief.   His griefs were uttered
the one after the other.   Afterwards he wandered,
sorrow-dazed, in time,   until the tide of death
approached his heart.   And the hoard? The old   2270
force, night-flyer,   found it undefended –
the seeker-out   of smouldering barrows,
smooth-scaled hate-dragon,   smithied in flame-work,
who flies at dark.   Those who dwell nearby
fear him, and with reason.   He's forced to search out   2275
the hoard in its earth,   and then the heathen gold
guard, endlessly,   ungraced by his watch.
   Three hundred years   this unhallowed harm
kept his eyes on   the cave of treasure,
mighty in his powers,   until a man handled   2280
the malice bred there,   bearing to his master
one plated flagon,   a peace-guarantee,
feud's settlement.   Once the site of treasure
had known pilfery,   pardon was granted
to the litigant,   and his lord could look   2285
for the first time on   that far-gathered glitter.
   But the worm stirred, and   new strife began:
he sniffed among stones,   scenting – implacable –
his enemy's smell,   whose secret craft
by stealth had disturbed   the strength waiting...   2290
(An undoomed man   may well survive

woes and miseries   if he's meritable,
bears the Lord's favour...)   Then, furious, the dragon
nosed out man-trace,   meaning to find
the one who'd troubled   his terrible dreams: 2295
shifted, enraged, through   the shape of his cavern,
to its outer ness.   No one was there
in that burnt fastness,   yet his blent evil
intended terror: at times he looked again
for the rifled cup,   only to discover again   2300
that someone already   had robbed him of the gold,
ancient treasure-token.   Until evening came
anxiously he waited,   waited wretchedly.
The enraged raptor,   rooked in his shelter,
would repay his foe   with fire, avenge   2305
the pilfered cup.   With departing day
the worm set to –   no intention now
of wallowing within his walls,   but to work in flames,
bright-scaled with fire.   His first assaults
were terrible, widespread –   and to the treasure-giver   2310
of that ailing land   it would end badly.
    Visitant, baleful,   the fire-storm braised
the bright farmsteads.   Flame-glow burned in
eyes everywhere;   this old enemy,
this force of air,   left few alive.   2315
The worm's war-trail   was widely seen,
his evil and malice.   Everywhere it was evident
how that purposeful harm   showed sheer hatred
to the Geat people.   And at the press of day
he'd rush back to   the abandoned hoard   2320
having torched skin to   scorching candles,
flesh-braided fire.   Only his far barrow and
war-cunning he'd trust: yet his trust gained him nothing.
    To Beowulf the terror   was told quickly,
with uttermost speed: his own throne-room,   2325

best of buildings,   had been burnt in battle,
Geatish treasure-well,   its good grief-stricken.
In thorough misery   his thoughts darkened.
The wise one believed   that the All-Wielder,
eternal Lord,   was treating him with contempt   2330
for some bitter offence.   His breast filled with
ailing thought-shadows   unlike himself.

   So the flame-dragon   had put to the fire
the tribe's stronghold,   torched its fortress,
razed the coastline.   The king, war-like,   2335
the Weders' chief,   chose only vengeance.
At his most lord-like   he commanded a shield –
all of iron,   intricately patterned
war-shelter – made.   Well he knew that   2340
fine-wrought lime-wood   wouldn't last fire-storms.
The brief life-flare   of that best of kings
was ending its days –   and the dragon's also,
whose lease on the hoard   had lasted so long.

   Fount of ring-gifts,   he refused to meet   2345
the air-scather   with any army
or assembled troop.   For himself he cared
nothing, nor dreaded   the dragon's war-craft,
its power or might.   Many times before
he'd been hard-pressed, had   had to survive in   2350
slaughter's chaos –   as when the kingly hall
of Hrothgar he'd cleansed,   keen in his triumph,
outmatching there   not only one monster
but the monster's kin.   In combat like that –
trials of hand-strength –   not least was the time   2355
when Hygelac was killed,   when the Geatish king,
his people's pride,   in the panic of war
perished in Friesland.   In fierce sword-slake
Hrethel's heir was slain,   hewn with bill-blades.
It was then Beowulf   breasted sea-strength: 2360

he came shorewards   carrying thirty
sets of war-gear,   seized as booty.
From him the Hetware   had joylessness.
Among their foot-soldiers,   in the solid shield-press
few exulted   and fewer returned   2365
to the kindness of home   from that killing-ground.
Then Ecgtheow's son,   solitary and sorrowing,
swam back again   over the sea's braiding
to Geatland. Hygd   offered him hoard, kingdom,
rings and treasure-seat.   She didn't yet trust Heardred –   2370
young heir unfit   to fend the throne
against foreign havoc   after Hygelac's death.
Yet there was no way   that the war-wasted
people could seek to   persuade Beowulf
to become their high leader,   lord over Heardred,   2375
to accept and keep   the offered kingdom.
He preferred to give   counsels of friendship,
to honour Heardred   until he grew older,
ruled the Weder-Geats.   But from that riven sea
Heardred was visited   by vicious exiles,   2380
bold Ohthere's sons,   who'd rebelled against
their Scylfing blood   and its best of kings –
the renowned lord who   lavished treasure-gifts
on the Swedish tribes.   It was trouble – the end –
for Heardred. Feast   turned to fury; swords   2385
cut at Hygelac's son,   caused his life-wound –
and afterwards the heir   of Ongentheow
sought home again   once Heardred was slain.
He allowed Beowulf –   best of chieftains –
to gain the throne   as Geat ruler.   2390
    For Heardred's death   he dealt vengeance
in future days: was Eadgils' friend
in friendlessness; sent   over the sea's edges
aid – men and weapons –   to Ohthere's heir;

afterwards visited   revenge in what were cold,   2395
difficult forays.   He brought Onela death.
   And so Ecgtheow's son   every setback
with capable courage   had countered, survived
all fierce feuding,   until the fateful day
he had to wage war on   the worm's hatred.   2400
One of twelve he went,   the Weder war-chief,
swollen with anger,   to seek the dragon.
By then he'd discovered   how this crime had arisen,
fateful to his people: the precious cup
had passed into his possession   from the pilferer's hand.   2405
He made the thirteenth   in Beowulf's troop,
the one who'd caused   this current trouble.
Sick at heart and   humbled, he scouted
the way to the place.   Unwillingly he went
to the unlustred cavern   he alone knew of,   2410
the barrow underground,   guarded by sea-whelm,
the fury of waves,   that was filled inside
with chased metalwork.   Its monstrous guard,
always war-ready,   had watched the gold
grow old under the earth.   It wasn't easily bought,   2415
cheap to access   for any clansman.
   On the wide headland,   wintered in slaughter
he sat, gold-giver   of the Geats, wishing
luck to his hearth-thanes.   His heart was dark,
restless, death-readied,   the doom closing   2420
which would at last attack   the tired veteran,
seek his soul-hoard   and tear asunder
life from its framing.   It wasn't for much longer
that Beowulf's flesh   would enfold his spirit.
   Beowulf, Ecgtheow's   offspring, then spoke: 2425
'In my youth, often   I yielded to nothing,
'survived everything.   I remember it all.
'Seven winters old,   I was sent away

'by my father, fostered   to the folk's treasure-lord.
'The king, Hrethel,   claimed and kept me   2430
'in kinship's ways –   kindness, treasure-feasts.
'As life went by   I was least in nothing,
'no less a chosen prince   than his own children –
'Herebeald or Hæthcyn   or Hygelac, my lord.
'Awful, accidental   that the eldest of them   2435
'sprawled on a deathbed   because of a kinsman's deed,
'after Hæthcyn strung   his horn-bound bow
'and buried a bolt   in his brother's body.
'He missed his shot,   murdering instead his
'older kinsman   with a blood-freaked arrow.   2440
'No wergild could be paid.   It was a profitless fight –
'meritless, meaningless.   A man – a prince –
'was deprived of life   and left unavenged.
    'This is the kind of sorrow   the soul of an old
'man comes to know   if his kin, his son   2445
'is swinging from the gallows.   Though there's grief, lament,
'death's mournful song,   his son hangs there
'and the raven gloats.   His great wisdom
'and age can do nothing;   there's nothing that can help.
'Every morning   he's reminded: his son   2450
'roams death-darkness.   In his dismal hall
'there's no sense waiting   for any second heir
'or inheritor   now the one has gone,
'has ended his deeds   in death's viciousness.
'Heart-stricken, he seeks   his son at his home: 2455
'sees the waste wine-hall,   wind-swept places
'emptied of happiness.   The horsemen have passed,
'heroes rot in earth.   No harp's struck or
'joy rings in yard   as joy did, once.
'He takes to his bed,   tells himself the grief-words: 2460
'alone; lonely.   Too large now every space,
'courtyard and plain.

'And so the Geatish king
'sorrowed for Herebeald,   his heart holding
'only welling sadness.   No way was there
'he could seek redress   from his son's slayer;   2465
'nor could he punish   the perpetrator –
'though no longer dear –   in deeds of revenge.
'In such a force of sorrow,   fallen on him so sadly,
'he gave up man's joys,   chose God's comfort,
'and like any blessed man   bequeathed to his heirs   2470
'land and township   after he'd left this life.

    'Once Hrethel had died,   hard enmity –
'criminal quarrelling,   commonplace violence –
'befell Swedes and Geats   on their stricken sea,
'and Ongentheow's sons   were able in war,   2475
'alert, active,   nor wished to live in peace
'across the holm's bonding.   Around Hreosnaburh
'time and again they   committed atrocities.
'Warriors – kin of mine –   for such cruel actions
'worked their vengeance,   as was widely known,   2480
'though one had to pay   the price of life:
'a dear bargain.   Doom threatened there
'the Geat princeling   in the press of war.
'I heard that in the dawn   one dear kinsman
'slaked his sword-edge   on the other's slayer...   2485
'there Eofor attacks   aged Ongentheow...
'war-helm slipped off...   The old Scylfing
'fell, deadly pale.   The fierce hand-work
'of old was recalled;   no cruelty was withheld.

    'To Hygelac I repaid   the plenty he'd given –   2490
'gold-treasures – in war.   War made my gift,
'and the lustred sword.   Land he gave me –
'home and homeland.   For him there was no need
'to get fighters   from the Goths or Danes,
'to seek and pay   Swedish hire-swords,   2495

'men more merciless   whose merits had their price.
'Always I'd be in the forefront,   first in the foot-ranks
'and fighting alone.   This too is my future –
'so to act in battle   while this blade can last,
'doing me service   as it's served of old,   2500
'as when I fetched, in   fierce hand-fighting,
'the Frankish doomsman   Dæghrefn from life
'in front of his troops.   To the Frisian king
'he could bring no bright,   breast-hung war-trinkets,
'but stricken he fell,   standard-bearer,   2505
'perished in his powers.   No polished sword-blade
'slew him. His heart-beat   ceased in my hand-crush,
'bone-house broke apart.   And now the same bill-edge,
'hands, forge-flamed sword   must fight for the hoard.'
      Beowulf then spoke   the vows of his spirit   2510
for the final time: 'I fought, once, in youth,
'risked many a combat;   in the coming conflict,
'and as the tribe's old Ward,   again I'll seek trial
'and shall act with courage   if that cruel ravager
'ever dares to come   from his den of earth.'   2515
He went to greet   his gathered men,
his beloved warriors,   lordly helm-bearers,
for the final time: 'No forcing sword
'or weapon I'd bear   against the worm-terror
'if I knew how to grapple him,   grind this monster   2520
'in a famous grip,   as I did once with Grendel,
'yet I expect nothing   but his poisonous breath,
'war-flame, hatred.   That's why I'm wearing
'shield and corselet.   Nor shall I yield
'one foot of ground   to this barrow's ward.   2525
'Fate, lord of all,   must make what befalls
'our twin futures.   I'm resolved – so firm
'that I won't waste more words   on the war-dragon.
'Here on this hilltop   you will have to wait,

'armed in war-tackle,   for which of we two   2530
'may survive better   the bitter wounding
'of our clamour-rush.   You can't claim this fight.
'It lies in no-one's power   but mine – alone,
'a measure of my strength   against monstrousness,
'my customary gift   of great courage.   2535
'I'll either win the gold   or war will claim
'your lord at last   in its life-shattering.'
  Up he straightened,   stern-faced, renowned,
helmeted, war-ready;   walked in battle-gear
towards the stone cliff-face.   He trusted his strength   2540
in single combat.   That was no coward's way.
  He'd survived many battles,   that best of men,
many keen conflicts   among clashing armies,
ranks of foot-soldiers.   Now he saw ramparts,
arches of stonework,   a stream breaking   2545
from the facing cliff.   It ran with flame's whelming,
heat's hate-currents.   The hoard he couldn't gain,
near without burning   for even the briefest time,
or endure dragon-flame   in those terrible depths.
Enraged, he gave   a great war-cry;   2550
lord of Weder-Geats,   he let anger
fly from his heart-storm.   The fury in his voice
echoed clearly   under the grey cliff-face.
Hatred was kindled: the hoard's guardian
heard a man's challenge;   there were no more chances   2555
to finick a peace.   At first, there came
from the stone buttress   the monster's breath,
hot battle-sweat.   The whole earth shook.
Fighting in the earth-barrow,   the First among Geats
swung rim, shield-edge   at the onrushing war-guest.   2560
Then the coiled thing's heart   was goaded, encouraged
to seek combat.   The king drew his
aged war-sword,   old inheritance

and keenest of edge. Each of the two was
intent on causing   most terror in the other.   2565
Keen and resolute,   the king stood firm,
a stern warlord   behind his steep-curved shield,
waiting in war-tackle   as the worm uncoiled.
Then it reared, and came   writhing, burning
and rushing towards fate.   His shield fended   2570
the attack on his life   for less time than
that dread leader   had dared to wish.
It was the first time ever   that Fate's judgement
fell on his fighting,   failed to win him
honour in combat.   Up went the sword-hand   2575
of the Geatish lord,   lashed at the terror-beast
with his ancient blade –   but the edge buckled;
its brightness bit   less keenly on bone
than the thanes' chieftain   had thought or hoped
in such a grim battle.   The barrow's guardian,   2580
its mind enraged   by such a mighty blow,
disgorged slaughter-flame   so that its glow lit up
the baleful land.   Here was no battle-boast
for the Geat gold-giver.   His great sword failed,
iron stripped of power;   such an old time-gift   2585
never should have done.   Here was no death-crossing
easy for far-famed   Ecgtheow's kinsman
as he prepared at last   to leave the world;
it was unwillingly   he went to inhabit
a home elsewhere,   yet so must every man   2590
leave his life-lease.   And before long, the two
mighty combatants   met once again.
The hoard-keeper's   heart was the keener,
welling with new effort.   He who'd once wielded
army and nation   ailed in the fire-storm.   2595
No close comrades   came rank-forming
around him. Those best   and bravest of men,

those choice fighters,   had fled to the forest
to save their skins.   Only a solitary one
felt sorrow's prompting: it's praiseworthy   2600
that kinship's claims   are kept in a man.
   He was called Wiglaf,   son of Weohstan,
trusted shieldsman   of the Scylfing tribe,
Ælfhere's kin.   He saw his aged lord
was maddened by the heat   of his battle-mask   2605
and remembered the gifts   granted by Beowulf
to the Wægmundings: wealth, dwelling-places,
folk-rights to commons –   as his father enjoyed.
There was no holding back: his hand seized shield,
yellow lime-wood's arc;   he drew his ancient sword,   2610
relic of Eanmund,   Ohthere's son,
in Weohstan's tribe.   Weohstan, wretched
in exile, turned slayer,   and in savage fighting
cut down Eanmund,   carrying to his kinsmen
blood-freaked helmet,   byrnie of chainmail   2615
and that giant-worked sword.   Onela's justice
returned to Weohstan   the war-tackle,
feud-mauled clothing –   yet of the feud, Onela
said nothing, though his brother's   son had been butchered.
Wiglaf's father   kept those fine treasures –   2620
mail-shirt and sword –   for many a year,
until his son in turn   matured in rank,
and later, among the Geats,   gave him countless
weapons and war-gear.   In wisdom and age
he found death's path.
                     This was the first foray   2625
where Wiglaf had been blooded,   when in the battle-rush
he'd had to stand   strong with his chieftain.
Nor did his courage melt,   nor that mighty sword
weaken in the war-play.   That was what the Worm discovered
after they'd clashed together   when combat came on.   2630

   Wiglaf then spoke   words fitting duty
to the men round him,   though he mourned in spirit.
'I remember a time   at the mead-sharing
'when we made a promise   to our mighty lord,
'best treasure-giver,   there in the beer-hall.   2635
'If force or need   befell him, we said,
'we'd want to repay   gifts of war-gear
'with hard blade, helm.   Because of that he had us
'chosen, hand-picked   for this hard venture.
'He judged us great,   gave me these treasures,   2640
'counted us with the bravest: bold helm-wearers
'and mace-bearers.   And although our lord had meant,
'as the tribe's Ward, to   take on alone
'and to carry out   this work of courage –
'since he's claimed among men   the most renown   2645
'for sheer daring –   now the day has come
'when our chief has need   of new-found strength,
'of good fighters.   Let us go to it,
'help our shield-leader   in that shining heat,
'grim flame-terror.   And for me, God knows   2650
'it's far better   that flame should swallow
'my body together   with my gold-giver.
'To me it's not right   that we should make for home
'with untested shields,   unless we've tried at first
'to kill this foe   and defend the life   2655
'of the Weders' lord.   I well believe
'he doesn't deserve,   given his deeds of old,
'to suffer alone,   sorrowful among the Geat-troop,
'and to fall in battle.   Together let us bid him
'a shared bale-shroud –   sword, byrnie and helm.'   2660
   Into the war-reek went   his war-helmet,
he to his leader's aid.   Few words he uttered:
'Dear-born Beowulf,   do everything now
'that you promised in youth,   years long ago:

'while you still lived, you said,   you would never allow   2665
'your doom to decay.   So now in the greatest deeds –
'princely, firm-spirited –   you must defend your life
'with all your powers.   I too shall aid you.'
 After Wiglaf's words   the Worm's anger
woke a second time.   Terrible, malicious,   2670
this fire-driven spirit   hurled itself forward
at his human foes.   Flame came in waves,
shield burnt to boss.   Nor did his byrnie
give any protection   to the good young man;
yet when his own shield-rim   had been eaten to ash   2675
he came forward,   fierce, unshaken,
behind his bondsman's shield.   And Beowulf then,
reminded of his strength,   struck out brutally,
swung his battle-bill   at the serpent's head –
but in need's violence   Nægling shattered.   2680
Beowulf's great sword,   grey-polished, ancient,
weakened in war-play.   It wasn't granted
that swords' edges   had been able, ever,
to help him fight.   His hand – or so I heard –   2685
was too strong; he   overstruck every
blood-hardened blade;   he was none the better for it.
 On a third attack   came the terror-creature,
the fire-scather,   more furious than before.
Once given room,   it rushed its attacker.   2690
Screaming with battle-heat   it clenched Beowulf's neck
between blade-sharp fangs;   he fell back, drowning
in the unending waves   of his own life-blood.
 I heard tell that   Wiglaf was true
in Beowulf's need.   He was bold, resolute,   2695
princely, fighting   alongside with natural power.
He paid no heed   to the creature's head.
He struck lower –   yet still his hand
in its courage was burnt   as he came to help,

to support his kinsman.   He plunged in his sword   2700
to its gold-stained hilt.   The dragon-fire began
to weaken. And again   Beowulf gathered
the last of his wits,   unleashing the knife –
sharp battle-biter –   he wore on his belt.
The Weder-Helm hacked   through the Worm's belly.   2705
Together the two   in their tireless courage
had felled the dragon,   had driven out his life
with twinned bravery.   So should a warrior be,
in the press of battle.

                        Yet for the prince it was
the last time his   deeds were to triumph   2710
in the world's working.   The mortal wound
the dragon gave him   afterwards began
to burn, to swell: soon Beowulf found
baleful battle-heat   blooming in his body –
a poison, spreading.   The prince slowly   2715
moved to the cliff-edge.   Calmed with wisdom,
on the rampart he sat,   seeing the giant-work,
how stone arches   on strong pillars
held up from within   an endless earth-hall.
Then Wiglaf, loyal   to the last, began   2720
to unlatch the clasp   on his lord's helmet –
his brave chieftain,   blood- and gore-spattered
and weary to death –   and to wash his face.
Beowulf then spoke,   in spite of his hurt,
war's mortal wound.   He knew full well   2725
the days of his life   were done, and done
their earthly joys: all, all was gone
of time's durance,   and death came on.
'It's to a son I'd give   these battle-garments,
'gore-stained war-trappings,   if I'd been granted   2730
'such an inheritor,   someone of my kin to
'outlast my corpse.   This clan I controlled

'for fifty snows.   No fellow-ruler –
'none surrounding,   none anywhere –
'dared once attack my   troops in their homeland,   2735
'or even threaten terror.   Time happened here
'while I waited, trying   to wield power well –
'no murderous treachery,   nor too many wrongful
'oaths came to pass.   There's pride in it all
'even here, when I'm weak,   wounded and mortal,   2740
'since the Prince of Men   can't reproach me, ever,
'for the murder of kin,   as my mortal body
'becomes a corpse.   Now quickly go
'to gaze on the hoard   under those grey arches,
'my best Wiglaf,   now the Worm lies dead   2745
'in a lethal sleep,   among the loss of treasure.
'Quick now, in haste,   so I might hold my eyes
'on the gold and look   on wealth's lustre,
'air-carved gem-stones.   It will be easier then
'to let go at last   and take my leave   2750
'of the life and land   I've kept so long.'
    I heard it said   that Weohstan's son,
having heard the words   of his wounded chief –
mortal, battle-sick –   bore himself away in
wire-wrought war-shirt   under the weathered arches.   2755
The youth looked in triumph   beyond the ledge;
the brave lad saw   jewels without limit,
gathered gold-work   glistering the earth-floor,
wondrous wall-hangings,   and the Worm's old den,
dawn-flier's lair,   loaded with flagons,   2760
lustreless silver   lacking its polishers,
dulled and tarnished.   There were upturned helmets,
old and rusted;   ancient arm-rings,
twisted with cunning.   So easily can treasure,
gold earthed in ground,   get the better of   2765
almost anyone,   whoever has hidden it.

While he looked, he saw   aloft over the hoard
the greatest of its treasures: a golden banner,
hand-linked, intricate.   By its ambient light
he could see further: the floor of the cavern,   2770
also piled with treasure.   No trace remained
of the Worm, stricken   and destroyed by the sword.
    I heard tell that   the treasure in the barrow,
work of giant-races,   was rifled by a man
who as the whim took him   loaded wine-cups and dishes   2775
into his arms. The banner   he took also,
most brilliant of things.

                Beowulf's knife-blade,
iron though it was, had   damaged and ended
the life of the one   who through long winters
warded those treasures,   whose welling fires   2780
flew in darkness,   dealt out savagery
in cruel midnights,   on account of the hoard.
    Wiglaf then tried   to return quickly,
made eager by the treasure,   yet he was anxious
in his fine spirit   whether he'd find his lord,   2785
wounded so badly,   still breathing there
in the place he'd left   not long before.
With his gathering of treasure   he found the great chieftain,
his own leader,   ailing, battle-bloodied,
his life almost spent.   Again he splashed   2790
his face with liquid,   until a final word
could break from his breast.   Beowulf then spoke,
glimpsing on Wiglaf   the garnered gold:
'For these treasures I thank   the Thinker of All,
'Maker Eternal,   with my mouth give praise   2795
'to the greatest Prince   for what I gaze on here,
'that I was able to endow   before my day of death
'all my people   with such old riches.
'Here I have paid for   this hoard of treasure

'with my life's passing.   My people's needs   2800
'you must look to.   I can't last longer.
'Order the battle-famed   to make a barrow,
'bright after my bale-fire –   a beacon on the cliff,
'mound and memorial   to my people,
'atop the high rock-fall   at Hronesness,   2805
'so that afterwards   to all sea-travellers
'far-scanning in ships   the fierce tideways
'it shall bear the name   of Beowulf's Barrow.'
   From his neck he took   a torc of gold,
that war-skilled prince,   gave it to Wiglaf,   2810
his good young friend,   with his gold helmet,
armour and bracelet,   said: 'Use them well.
'You're last in the line   of long kinship,
'of fine Waegmundings.   Fate's swept away
'my valiant clan   in their virtues and powers   2815
'to judgement in death.   I'm due to follow.'
It was the last utterance,   old one's heart-thought,
final leave-taking   before fire's mettling
and its hot seething.   Soul reft away,
found a less brutal   and a better justice.   2820
   It went hard then   with the young warrior,
as wretchedly he watched   his dear ring-giver
there on the earth while   his life ended
in such misery.   His slayer, too, lay dead:
land-dragon destroyed,   the strife-bringer   2825
still and lifeless.   No longer could the Worm's
uncanny writhings   keep the ring-hoard;
iron sword-edges,   age-old battle-shards,
relics of forge-hammers,   had reft it of life,
and the cloud-flier's   corpse lay on dirt,   2830
was stiffening in death   near its den and hoard.
No longer would he fly –   a fury in air –
in midnight's pride,   preening in his power

and greed for treasure,   but was hacked to ground
by Beowulf's hard   hand-strength in battle.   2835
I've heard of few   fighters anywhere,
even among the most daring   in every deed,
even among mankind's   mightiest and greatest,
who would have rushed and braved   spewing breath-poison
or gone to pillage   the great ring-hall,   2840
finding its warden   alive and watchful,
occupying its barrow.   There Beowulf's share,
his portion of treasures,   was paid for in death.
Each of them had come to   their end, had been fetched
from their loan of life.

                        It wasn't long afterwards   2845
that the battle-slackers   slunk from the forest,
weak truth-breakers,   ten told together –
the cowards, who'd failed   to fight earlier
or launch their spears   in their lord's great need.
Ashamed now, they came,   carrying their shields   2850
and war-gear, where   their war-chief lay dead,
and found Wiglaf.   Worn out, he sat,
a lone foot-soldier,   near his lord's shoulders,
hoping uselessly   to help him with water.
However well he meant,   no man on earth   2855
could ever have preserved   the old one's life
or change what God   had chosen already:
it was God's judgement   that would rightly govern
the deeds of every man,   as it still does today.

    When one of the cowards spoke,   a cutting answer   2860
came back quickly   from the brave young man.
Wiglaf, the son   of Weohstan, spoke
from grief's spirit   to the gutless ones:
'Speak truthfully   if you can speak the truth.
'Say that your great chieftain – who gave you treasures,   2865
'even the war-tackle   that you're wearing now,

'who on the mead-benches,   a prince among his men,
'gifted to so many   of the hall-muster
'helmet and corselet,   the costliest and best
'to be found anywhere,   far-flung or near –   2870
'utterly wasted   war-gifts and gear,
'had lavished them in vain   when violence came.
'In no manner could   the king ever boast
'of comrades in his ranks.   Yet the Ruler, God,
'allowed him to triumph,   to take revenge   2875
'with his lone knife-edge   when he most needed courage.
'There was little aid   I could bring him
'or protection in war,   though I tried to fight
'beyond my powers   to help my prince.
'When I drove my sword   into the dragon's fierceness   2880
'the foe weakened.   Flame welled less strong
'from its fire-livid head.   Yet too few defenders
'gathered round the leader   in his greatest peril.
'And now your treasure-getting,   the gifting of swords,
'your joy in clan,   in kin and home,   2885
'will have to stop.   Each man will be stripped –
'down to each relative,   each wrecked family –
'of his right to land   after royal leaders
'from afar shall hear   of just how you fled,
'were worthless in deed.   Death is better   2890
'than living for any man   living so shamefully.'
     The fighting's end   and outcome he ordered
told at the encampment   atop the cliff-edge.
For that whole morning   men of war had
waited, shield-wearers   unsure whether the news   2895
would be of Beowulf's death   or the dear return
of their beloved lord.   He held little back,
the rider who took   the sad tidings,
but loudly called out   in everyone's hearing:
     'Now the wish-granter   of the Weder tribe,   2900

'lord of Geats, is⠀⠀limb-fast in death.
'The Worm's hatred⠀⠀holds him in death-sleep.
'That life-taker⠀⠀lies beside him,
'killed by knife-blades.⠀⠀His sword could not
'find any purchase,⠀⠀inflict any wound⠀⠀⠀⠀⠀⠀⠀2905
'on the loathsome thing.⠀⠀Wiglaf's alive,
'and Weohstan's son⠀⠀sits by Beowulf,
'the living grieving⠀⠀one now lifeless.
'Weary, mind-darkened,⠀⠀death's watch he keeps
'over the loved and loathed.⠀⠀Now what looms over us,⠀⠀2910
'once Beowulf's fall⠀⠀is far noticed
'among the Frisians and Franks,⠀⠀is war's fury.
'It was framed by Franks,⠀⠀that fierce quarrel,
'after Hygelac went⠀⠀in wound-necked ships
'to attack Friesland⠀⠀with his fleet and troops.⠀⠀⠀⠀2915
'The Hetware⠀⠀hounded and attacked him,
'he was outnumbered,⠀⠀overcome in battle,
'the mailed fighter⠀⠀was forced to submit,
'falling in the foot-troop.⠀⠀No follower got treasures
'from this honoured lord.⠀⠀Ever afterwards⠀⠀⠀⠀⠀2920
'the Frankish king⠀⠀showed us no kindness.
⠀⠀'Nor from the tribe of Swedes⠀⠀can truce or peace
'ever be expected.⠀⠀Everywhere it's known
'that Hæthcyn, son⠀⠀of Hrethel, was killed
'by royal Ongentheow⠀⠀near Ravenswood⠀⠀⠀⠀⠀2925
'when Geat forces⠀⠀had first in their pride
'attacked the Swedes,⠀⠀tribe of Scylfings.
'Ohthere's father,⠀⠀aged in wisdom
'and terrifying in war,⠀⠀returned the attack.
'He despatched Hæthcyn,⠀⠀so sparing the life⠀⠀⠀⠀2930
'of his own woman,⠀⠀old and ring-bereft,
'mother of Onela⠀⠀and of Ohthere,
'afterwards hunting⠀⠀the hostile troops
'until they escaped by⠀⠀the skin of their teeth,

'running, leaderless,   into Ravenswood.   2935
'Wretched sword-remnant,   they were surrounded
'and wound-wearied.   Down the widths of night,
'often Ongentheow   offered them miseries,
'said that when morning broke   their blood would flow
'from cutting sword-edge,   or they'd be claimed by gallows,   2940
'death-bloated birds.   But when daybreak came
'the sorry-spirited   had some comfort
'when they heard Hygelac's   horn-blast, the sound
'of yelling trumpets,   as he trailed them,
'a hero on their track   with his most trusted men.   2945
    'It was seen everywhere,   war's slaughter-rush,
'the blood-swath scythed   between Swedes and Geats,
'the growth of the feud   gathering between their peoples.
'And Ongentheow,   old and sorrow-mettled,
'retreated with his troop   and tribe to a place   2950
'more secure, on   the climbing ground.
'Of Hygelac he'd heard – his hardened skill,
'tireless war-cunning.   He didn't trust his own –
'that he could oppose   plundering sea-troops,
'safeguard the hoard,   save wife and children   2955
'from the battle-ravagers.   So back he fell,
'behind an earth-wall.   Then Hygelac advanced
'on the Swedish tribe,   his banners tracking
'across the surrounding plain   to their hiding place
'after the Hrethlings had pressed   towards that high refuge.   2960
'There Ongentheow,   old and grey-haired,
'was brought to bay   by battle-swords
'until this fierce chieftain   was forced to suffer
'Eofor's own justice.   Out of anger, Wulf –
'Wulf Wonreding –   had wielded his weapon   2965
'so that the brutal blow   set blood streaming
'from Ongentheow's hair.   Yet the old Scylfing
'still felt no fear,   and furiously repaid

'the war-onslaught   with one even worse:
'the king had turned   there on his attacker.   2970
'Nor could Wonred's son,   however resourceful,
'offer a counterblow   to the aged man.
'Wulf's head was carved   to his helmet's width
'and he staggered, bowed   under flowing blood,
'then fell to the earth.   (He was still unfated: 2975
'though the wound was deep,   he did recover.)
'And Eofor, in fury,   following Hygelac,
'saw his brother cut down.   With his broad war-sword –
'hand-work of giants –   he hacked through the shield,
'carved at the helmet.   Then the king buckled: 2980
'steward of his people,   he was struck from life.
'Afterwards, there were many   who helped Eofor's brother;
'they treated his wounds,   tended and lifted him,
'once their band controlled   that blood-drenched spot.
'Eofor, meanwhile,   stripped Ongentheow,   2985
'robbed him of war-gear,   the wrought corselet,
'hard, hilted sword,   and the battle-helmet,
'carrying these relics   to Hygelac the king.
'When he got these treasures   he made a great promise
'to Eofor and his clan   of bounty – and kept it: 2990
'after his homecoming,   the king of the Geats,
'Hrethel's offspring,   paid Eofor and Wulf
'lavishly for their exploit   in priceless loot,
'gifting each of them   with extensive lands
'and numberless rings –   no man on middle-earth   2995
'could reproach them for such gifts,   since they'd gained them by
                                                                                fighting –
'and also to Eofor   giving his own daughter,
'an honour to his home,   as amity's pledge.
    'And that is the feud –   fierce enmity,
'unfinished slaughter –   I sorrow about,   3000
'which will cause the tribe   of Swedes to attack

'as soon as they've heard   that our high lord lies
'with his life taken,   who always protected
'our land and assets   against all enemies
'and after the heroes' fall   among the fierce Scyldings   3005
'aided a whole people,   further practicing
'whole-hearted valour.

           And now haste is best:
'we should go to look   at our great chieftain,
'our ring-giver,   and grieve him on his way
'to the funeral pyre.   No part of the treasure,   3010
'the massive hoard,   shall remain unmelted:
'that countless gold,   so cruelly bought,
'and numberless rings,   are now at the last
'paid for with his passage.   The pyre will eat,
'flame enfold them: no fighter shall wear   3015
'treasures as tokens,   no attractive girl
'have a ring-necklace   resting on her shoulders.
'Lost, pain-stricken,   deprived of the gold,
'often they'll wander   down exile's ways
'now their leader is dead   and his laughter, pleasure   3020
'and happiness doomed.   Many a dawn-cold spear,
'therefore, shall be wrapped   in fighters' fists,
'raised and brandished;   it's not the ringing harp
'that shall wake warriors   but the war-glutted raven
'busy over corpses,   his baleful voice   3025
'telling the eagle   how avidly he choked
'as he and the wolf   ate the war-offal.'
    The hateful tale   was told in full
by the brave messenger.   His meanings were blunt
and all came true.   The troop got up   3030
and went trailing,   with welling tears,
to see Earnaness   with their own eyes.
They found him on the sand,   where his soul had fled.
Their ring-giver   of old now ruled

only a death-bed.   In this end of time,   3035
as greatness passed,   their good leader,
the lord of the Weders,   had met a wondrous death.
But first their eyes rested   on a rarer thing:
there opposite them,   the Worm – upturned,
evil, lying dead.   The flame-dragon,   3040
streaked, soot-mottled,   had been stained by fire.
Stretched out, fifty   foot-marks he told,
when measured to his end.   Air-pleasured, he ruled
midnights' spaces,   spiralled downwards
to enter his den.   He lay still in death,   3045
had used the last   of his earth-barrows.
Around him were piled   plates and goblets,
dishes and beakers   and dear-bought swords –
all rusted through,   as if the earth-deep
had held such wealth   a thousand winters.   3050
But this vast legacy   had a living power,
its spoils and its gold   held there spell-bound:
no-one could touch   the trove of rings
unless God Himself,   Great King of Truth,
mankind's Guardian,   granted and allowed him   3055
– as a man worthy   and most of merit –
power to open   the ancient hoard.

    And so it was seen   that there was no success
for the unhallowed one   who'd wrongly hidden
the trove in the ground;   its guardian slew   3060
that man, among others;   and then this old feuding
was fiercely settled.   However famed the man,
no-one knows how fate   will fetch him to the end
of his life-shaping   when he can no longer
live in the mead-hall   with his men and kin.   3065
So it was with Beowulf,   when he sought the barrow-warden
and its vile hatreds;   how his visit to the world
would end was still   unknown to him.

It was princes of old   who first placed the hoard
and who laid a curse   lasting till doomsday: 3070
what man so ever   despoiling the mound
would be guilty of wrongs,   was greatly to be punished –
exiled among heathens,   chained in hell-bands.
Yet Beowulf's glimpse   of time's gold-treasures
wasn't at all greedy   or over-eager.   3075
　　Wiglaf, the son   of Weohstan, spoke:
'*If one man's wilful,   many others must*
'*endure exile*.   This has befallen us.
'By no counsel   or claim could we advise
'our beloved chieftain,   our land's warden,   3080
'not to go to meet   the gold-guardian
'but to let him lie   where he'd lived so long,
'waiting in his earth-halls   until the world ended.
'He held to his high purpose,   and the hoard's open,
'gifted so grimly.   That he was granted   3085
'to go there at all   was an awful fate.
'Once my way was clear   I went inside,
'and saw everything   in the armour-strewn hall –
'getting under the earth-wall   was ground gained with
'no sweetness at all.   In haste, I seized   3090
'a freight of treasure,   a whole fortune,
'in my hands, and bore   the booty outside
'to where Beowulf lay.   He was still living.
'Wise in his spirit   he spoke of much,
'aged and grieving,   asking me to greet you,   3095
'commanding you to make   in remembrance of his deeds
'a high-built barrow   above his burning-place,
'one as gloriously great   as his own greatness –
'the most worthy   of warriors among men,
'most widely renowned   in the world for honour.   3100
'Let's go now in haste   again under the wall,
'to witness that pile   of precious gem-stones,

'shining treasure-heap.   I'll show you the way,
'so you'll be close enough   to see clearly
'the broad gold-swath.   And let a bier be readied –   3105
'do it quickly,   for when we come outside –
'and then let us carry   our clan's chieftain,
'beloved of men,   to where at last he'll rest
'in the long keeping   of the Lord of All.'
    Then Weohstan's son,   warrior and hero,   3110
directed the tribe –   townsmen, house-holders,
and the heads of clans –   to carry firewood,
to fetch it from afar   to the funeral pyre
and its freight of good: 'Now flame will eat
'with its waxing tongue   our warrior lord,   3115
'who often endured   the iron-shower,
'the strings' power   as the arrow-storm fell,
'shocking the shield-wall,   each shaft true-tracked,
'each feather following   the flight of the barb.'
    Then Weohstan's son   wisely selected   3120
from among the closest   of the king's war-thanes,
summoning seven all told,   the best of the troop.
He went as the eighth   under the enemy's roof –
warriors into battle.   Walking before them,
one bore in his hands   a flaming brand.   3125
There was no lottery   for who should loot the hoard
after these few saw it   undefended,
without any guardian –   unprotected,
lying vulnerable.   And little did they mourn
when they quickly fetched   the fabled treasures   3130
out into daylight.   The dragon, too, they dumped,
ditching it down a cliff-face,   letting the clabber of waves,
toiling tide-reaches   have their trinket-lover.
The precious gold-work –   each piece priceless –
they loaded on a wagon,   and carried their lord,   3135
their hoar-grey chief,   to Hronesness.

    The people of the Geats   then prepared for him
a fitting and proper   funeral barrow
hung with helmets,   hued with battle-shields,
with bright corselets,   just as he'd requested.   3140
In its midst they laid   their mighty prince,
lamenting their beloved   lord and protector.
Grieving warriors   began to kindle
the pyre, built huge   on the high headland.
Smoke climbed and scattered   as swart wood caught   3145
in a crackle of flame,   whose call mingled
with their tide of cries –   a tumult, dying
only when his body's core   broke, fire-eaten.
That death they grieved   with dirges, sorrow,
one death-lay sung   by a woman, who...   3150
    ...   with hair bound up...
sang grief's concern,   whose song expressed
her fear that time   would fill with terror –
vicious invasion,   vile kidnap, killing,
humiliation.   Heaven swallowed the smoke.   3155
Then those stricken people   constructed a place
on the headland's heel –   high-sheltered, broad,
visible to the horizon,   to those viking seas.
Ten days they built   this beacon, sign
of their lord's courage.   Round what was left of ashes   3160
they built a wall,   as well and splendidly
as their cleverest men   could conceive it.
Into the mound they carried   the collars and jewels –
all the adornments   which envious hands
had once stolen   from the wondrous hoard.   3165
They let earth hold those   ancient treasures,
left gold to the ground,   where again it rests,
useless, unprofitable,   as once before.
Twelve warriors rode   around the mound.
Known for bravery,   of noble descent,   3170

they would claim and name   their numberless griefs,
utter in memory   an elegy for their king.
Stewardship they praised;   his strength and valour;
they mourned and assessed   his many virtues.
Fitting it is that   his fellows should praise   3175
a man's memory   and merits with love
once his spirit's been fetched   from its frame of life.
And so they lamented,   these men of the Geats –
companions and brothers –   the passing of their lord.
They said that of all   earthly rulers   3180
he'd been the mildest man,   and the most gentle,
kindest to his clansmen,   and keenest in fame.

AFTERWORD

OCCASIONALLY I HAVE NIGHTMARES whose theme is the present more-or-less metrical translation of *Beowulf*. In such nightmares I'm sitting in a well-appointed study-room – it might be in an Oxbridge college – and facing me across a highly polished table (on which lie carefully annotated imprints of the latest philological journals) is an interlocutor. It is of indeterminate gender, this interlocutor. S/he is a compound of the greatest scholars I have known and s/he wears the adjective 'formidable' as easily I would wear my watch. S/he is not unkind; s/he is merely and genuinely curious. S/he speaks.

'And why, Dr McCully,' (I note glumly that we must use titles), 'did you decide to translate *Beowulf*?'

'Well...,' I hesitate (tacitly adding a Sir or Professor, or possibly a Madam). 'Well, I was in Greenland, you see... In a tent...'

'In... a tent?' (rising intonation; incredulity: Margaret Rutherford's '... handbag?')

Pause.

That went well, I think, in my nightmare.

'And I see,' s/he continues (scanning the opening lines of text), 'that you have chosen *somewhat* to evade the question as to the extrametricality or otherwise of the opening word of the poem, *Hwæt*. Why did you do so?'

'Er... I fudged it. Some*hwæt*.'

'And the notable textual crux provided by lines 178a–180b – the lineation from, of course [of course], Klaeber's great edition of the poem? How did you treat of that particular theme?'

'Er... I fudged it,' I say. Clammily.

'And again,' (remorseless) 'the metrical problem posed *inter alia* by the lineation of half-lines 1165b to 1168b? How did you incorporate hypermetricality into your translation?'

'Well, I fudged it... er, *inter alia*.' Definitely sweating.

Pause.

That went a bit less well, I think, in my nightmare.

'And finally,' (finally sounds good), 'how in your new work did you solve the perennial problem for a contemporary translator of the unavoidable interplay between Germanic and Romance diction?'

'I'm afraid...'

Time taps its foot. Silence. A clock ticks out the syllables *Tolkien, Tol-kien*. In the blown bush outside the college window there's the laughing alarm call of a blackbird: *Hea-ney-did-it-ha-ha-ha*.

'I'm afraid that I fudged it.'

WHAT?

An afterword of this kind is helpful if it tries to answer three questions as honestly as possible: What? How? and Why? *What* kind of poem is *Beowulf*? *How* did the translator go about his business (that is, how did the fudging take place)? And *why* did the translator go about his business in the way he did?[1]

What kind of poem is *Beowulf*? It's tempting to say immediately that *Beowulf* is an epic, a tragic epic. Yet it was Tolkien, in what is still one of the best essays on the poem, who cautioned that *Beowulf* 'may turn out to be no epic at all' (1936, p.12). In fact, Tolkien went so far as to claim that Beowulf 'is not an "epic", not even a magnified "lay"' (1936, p.33). Yet I myself believe, as other translators have believed (see for example Alexander, 1973), that *Beowulf* is an epic poem, and I should here justify that belief.

---

1 I refer to the translator as 'he' and use the corresponding possessive pronoun 'his' merely because I am writing in the present instance largely of my own relationship with, and practices regarding, *Beowulf*.

The *Oxford English Dictionary* (OED) is curiously circular about the term epic, which it defines as:

> [p]ertaining to that species of poetical composition (see EPOS) represented typically by the *Iliad* and *Odyssey*, which celebrates in the form of a continuous narrative the achievements of one or more personages of history or tradition.

The OED gives the first attestation of the word's occurrence in English to Puttenham, astonishingly late in the history of English letters, in 1589.[2]

The definition seems unsatisfactory: 'X is a poem in a continuous narrative. The *Odyssey* has [arguably] a continuous narrative. The *Odyssey* is an epic. Therefore X is an epic.' Much here depends on what 'continuous' means. If it means 'chronologically uninterrupted' then even that 'typical' epic, the *Odyssey*, shows distressing signs of discontinuity, particularly in those episodes – episodes so vital to any oral teller of tales – of flashback and recapitulation. Further, the definition is problematic if applied to, for example, *Paradise Lost*. Who is the protagonist of *Paradise Lost*? If Satan, what business has the poet 'celebrating his achievements' in an epic poem? If Christ, then Christ's achievements, however they might be celebrated, are among the least poetically convincing things found within Milton's great poem.

If its definition of epic is at best problematic, the OED nevertheless offers the further instruction to 'see EPOS'. Accordingly, I saw EPOS:

---

2 George Puttenham's *Arte of English Poesie*, 1589. Puttenham's treatise, along with work by his contemporaries, was edited by G. Gregory Smith (*Elizabethan Critical Essays*, Oxford: Clarendon Press, 1904) and is available online: http://www.bartleby.com/359/

[a] collective term for early unwritten narrative poems celebrating incidents of heroic tradition; the rudimentary form of epic poetry.

That's sense 1a. Sense 2 defines *epos* as 'a series of events worthy of heroic treatment'. But it is not clear whether the treatment of this series of events should be in a continuous narrative; nor is it clear whether, if epic relate to epos, all non-oral poetic compositions would be debarred from being epics, however thoroughly they might receive the 'heroic treatment'; nor is it at all clear what 'heroic treatment' actually means.

Problems of definition multiply if we try to identify those works that are epic and distinguish them from those that are not. In a Scandinavian context, is the *Kalevala* an epic – or a collection of fantasy and folk-tale? In an English context, and if epic is related to relative length alone, are the *Canterbury Tales*, taken together, an epic? Is Malory's *Morte* an epic? Is *Gawain* – or is *Gawain* what I would myself wish to argue it is, a romance? Is *Paradise Lost* an epic? Is Wordsworth's *The Prelude*? Is *The Ring and the Book*? Are the *Cantos*? Of modern and contemporary works, and while it's clear that Walcott's *Omeros* (1990) is explicitly an epic, are Olson's *Maximus* poems? Is Muriel Rukeyser's 'The Book of the Dead' (which one dear colleague claimed was written in, and from, 'the epic mood') an epic? Is Lisa Robertson's *Debbie: An Epic* (1997) an epic? And really, even given that the prior candidates are all poems, must an epic really be set in verse? If not, then is *Middlemarch* an epic? Is *Lord of the Rings*? Is *Game of Thrones*, for all its epic qualities, and probably its epic aspirations, an epic?

When we consider *Beowulf* specifically, problems of definition become ever more acute. It's useful, for instance, to have the views of Milton's contemporaries to the effect that Milton was an epic poet; we can also trace the grosser structure(s) of *Paradise Lost* (by which I mean its authorial and editorial division into first ten, then twelve, books) to Lucan and to Virgil (see Hurley and O'Neill 2012, p.128), and Milton's statement of his own poetic ambition as well as his invocation of his epic-writing precursors, notably Homer, helps us locate *Paradise Lost* in a world of epic conventions – however those conventions are surpassed, subverted or ironised by the poem. Similarly, we know *something* of Chaucer's life and work that would probably make us wish to say that, despite their total length, the *Canterbury Tales* are just that – tales, some of which look back to the French *fabliau* tradition, others to Boccaccio and his reworking of troubadour materials. Yet of *Beowulf* we know nothing comparable. The authorship of the poem is unknown. Its origins clearly lie in story materials familiar in the remote pasts of the peoples who spoke dialects of the North and/or West Germanic languages of what is now Europe, but precisely when and how these story materials were incorporated into a single poem is unknown. The ultimate English provenance of the poem – Wessex? Mercia? – is unknown. The precise composition of its original audiences is unknown. It's quite true that much more is known about these matters than was the case when I first encountered the poem at the end of the 1970s but *Beowulf* in many ways remains a mystery. Yet I still believe it's an epic.

A look for other, and if possible concise, definitions of epic may help us forward. Lennard's *Poetry Handbook* (2005), contrasting epic with lyric, suggests that epic 'refers to long narratives collected from oral tradition and literary imitations of them; the process of imitation […] has created tremendous diversity, but the central idea of dealing with group-history and identity is strong enough to persist in diminutive forms such as the epyllion' (2005, p.66). The same work amplifies in its glossary, where epic is described as 'a classical mode […] usually dealing with the heroic or martial exploits of a person, tribe, or race, and [is] associated with nation-founding scale' (p.369). 'Nation-founding scale' is clearly true of the *Aeneid*, less certainly true of the *Odyssey*, though in those respective epics there is a highly significant recurrence of themes of *justice, effective governance* and *appropriate conduct* – particularly the conduct of the protagonist.

The *Princeton Encyclopedia of Poetry and Poetics* offers no concise definition of epic, yet usefully offers an extended survey of what epics have been, or have been held to have been. 'Virgil's *Aeneid*,' it writes, 'is a creative imitation of the *Iliad* and the *Odyssey*, but [...] [i]t is deliberately conceived, as they had not been, to give meaning to the destiny of a people, asserting the implications of their history and recognizing the significance of contemporary events in relation to the past' (p.243). Strangely, in what is otherwise a magisterial survey, the *Princeton Encyclopedia* says nothing specific to *Beowulf* under its entry for epic, although it does briefly mention oral epic song and the formulaic structures so often held to be parts of oral-formulaic composition and recitation (p.246).

Hurley and O'Neill (2012, p.120ff.) admirably concentrate on some formal properties of and conventions pertaining to the epic, such as the form's 'cultural concern with heroism' and the Classical epic convention of beginning *in medias res* (p.120). Yet they also stress that in the *Aeneid*, for example, the poem's theme of nation-founding is accompanied by an emphasis on 'the cost of these imperatives for the hero' (p.121). Heroic action, however courageous, is accompanied by *consequences* ('Aeneas must renounce Dido [...]; he quells his feelings, but the consequence is that she takes her own life' p.121). Those consequences may be both personally and societally tragic – a term I'll try to explore later.

None of these works say much, if anything, about *Beowulf*. I suspect that may be because *Beowulf* exists in a cultural milieu as far from Classicism as might at first blush be conceived. It's entirely possible to construct – many have constructed – a plausible and interesting genealogy of epic that runs from Homer through Plato to Virgil, Horace and later canonical authors such as Spenser, Milton and Wordsworth, all (with the possible exception of Homer) working in traditions of reactive literacy. Yet somehow *Beowulf*, like the *Hildebrandslied* and the *Kalevala*, seems to exist (that is, many appear to think these texts exist) in a quite different, orally inspired tradition. Even though Tolkien rightly rejected the term 'lay' for

Beowulf, the phrase 'heroic lay' still plays about these texts, as if somehow their presumed song-like nature debars them from participating in a literate and central (Classical) European tradition. Of course, even if *Beowulf* is an epic, it's an epic unlike the *Aeneid*, but too much can be and is made of 'singers of tales' – one senses a disapproving sniff at these no doubt skilled but nevertheless odoriferous and long-haired no-goods – and the 'oral-formulaic' diction held to be part of the Germanic process of poetic composition. It is not accidental, for example, that yesterday I found myself reviewing a paper for one of the learned journals which suggested that 'alliterative poems, such as *Beowulf* [...] or *Sir Gawain and the Green Knight*' were 'probably composed and delivered orally'. One notices the spectacular appearance of the word 'probably'.

My view is this: however it or some of its themes and episodes may have begun life in song, *Beowulf* as we know it is not a song, nor even a 'heroic lay'. It's quite true that there's a long and distinguished scholarly tradition, beginning in Germany in the late nineteenth century, that with persistence ascribes temporal (song-like) internal structure to *Beowulf* (Heusler 1891; Pope 1942 [1966]; Creed 1966, 1990; Obst 1987, 1996). Of these theories of composition and delivery, none has been more influential than that of Pope, who ingeniously postulated that the presumed isochronic nature of *Beowulf*'s language was carried in rhythmical beats signalled by harp-strokes. (In this tradition, too, I could once have placed myself: long ago I very much wanted *Beowulf* to behave like a song and recall trying to reconstruct a metre for *Beowulf* that included isochrony and silent off-beats as underlying, structural elements of the poem.) Why, given this freight of scholarship, would I want to argue against it?

The devil is, as always, in the detail. Students of the poem will be familiar with a constraint called *resolution*. Under resolution, a short, stressed syllable followed by a single consonant and a following, unstressed syllable may behave metrically as if the resolved syllables are equivalent to one long, stressed syllable. Thus

*freme*don in *ellen fremedon* (*Beo* 3b; 'performed (acts of) courage')
is conventionally said to be resolved: the initial syllable is short and
stressed; the vowel is followed by one and only one consonant; and
that consonant is followed by an unstressed syllable. In the same
half-line, however, *ellen* is not resolved: the initial stressed syllable
is followed by two consonants (a geminate, symbolised by <ll>)
and thus can't participate in resolution. The function of resolution
is, like the functions of contraction, parasiting, and syncopation,
to provide, as Terasawa points out, an artificial (i.e. verse-specific)
mechanism whereby the poet 'can adjust the number of syllables to
fit half-lines into acceptable rhythmical patterns' (Terasawa 2011,
p.55; see also Fulk 1992, p.153ff.).

It's just about conceivable that a singer might be able to adjust his or her output spontaneously, syllable-by-syllable, so that
the song fitted an 'acceptable' – one supposes, in this instance,
isochronic – pattern. And phrases such as *ellen fremedon* can of
course be produced isochronically, with beats on the initial syllables of both lexemes and a little hop on *freme-*. So the existence of
resolution is in itself no crucial argument against more or less spon-
taneous oral composition or musically orientated performance. My
friend and colleague Grevel Lindop also points out that the binary
distinction between 'song' and 'speech' may be simplistic, noting
that 'there can be more or less musical readings of both prose and
verse'.[3] I can myself conceive of readings of *Beowulf* that include
forms of chanting, possibly with harp accompaniment. I can also
conceive of readings in which the poet or reciter produced resolved sequences of syllables quite intuitively. Even then, however,
I wouldn't wish to claim that the poem had its genesis in music or
in song – nor in spontaneously-generated, intuitive renderings of its
narrative matter. The text as we have it seems – to me, at least, and
for what it's worth – too bookish, too literate and carefully worked

---

3 Personal communication, 20 December 2017.

for that. So the *takttheorie* remains unproven, though promising and challenging.

Less easy to explain for any *takttheorie*, however, are the many instances in the poem where resolution appears to be suspended (see Fulk 1992, p153ff.) The word *–locan*, for example, evident in a half-line such as *bāt bānlocan* (Beo 742a: 'bit into the bone-locks'[joints]) would under different circumstances be a candidate for resolution, yet here is unresolved. Were the syllables to be re-solved, the resultant half-line would have only three metrical po-sitions against the normative four (on abstract metrical positions, see *How?* below). Terasawa, in a very clear description of the phe-nomenon, points out that resolution in *Beowulf* may be suspended under two conditions:

    a) where the potentially resolvable sequence is preceded by a stressed and long syllable in the same metrical constituent

    b) where the resolvable sequence has a minimally bimoraic second syllable

In Beo. 278a, *þurh rūmne sefan*, 'from a generous mind', *sefan* would be resolved even though its final syllable was bimoraic *(-an)* because it is not preceded by a stressed and long syllable in the same metrical foot *(rūm-* is separated from the potentially resolv-able sequence by the inflection *–ne*). In Beo. 742a, *–locan* is un-resolved because it is preceded within the same metrical foot – a constituent that here spans a compound word – by a long, stressed syllable *(bān-)*.

If this constraint on resolution is correct then it's difficult to imagine it being observed in the circumstances surrounding spon-taneous recitation. I am not, after all, usually aware of the vowel lengths or syllabic compositions of the words I'm speaking at any given moment. I doubt many if any users of spoken language are so aware. The constraint seems to suggest not spontaneous impro-visation on the harp but rather, a highly wrought, specialised *and scriptist* language. Far from being what Edith Sitwell, in a quote I'm too idle to hunt down, called 'crude and unskilled thumping', the *Beowulf* metre seems intricate, elegant – and in its awareness of syllabic quantity, stress and syllabic adjacencies, to smell of parchment and scribal candlegrease.

There are two other arguments against the ascription of song-like-ness to *Beowulf*. The first is this. Pope's work – great, ingenious, provocative – depends largely on the assumption that Old English could be isochronous in the same way as later Englishes. Yet present-day isochrony allows for, indeed demands, that under certain circumstances lexical monosyllables, which would otherwise bear full stress, may be perceived as less stressed than surrounding words so that isochrony may be maintained (thus, in a high-level periodicity, *blind* in e.g. *three blind mice*). It also requires that some function words may be promoted to relative stress – again so that isochrony may be maintained or, more cautiously, so that the pressure to maintain isochrony may be felt by speaker and reader (thus *to* in *Shall I compare thee to a summer's day?*) Isochrony, that is, disfavours consecutive, equally stressed monosyllables just as it disfavours long runs of unstressed syllables. There's evidence in *Beowulf* and other Old English poems that stressed monosyllables may function metrically as equivalent to unstressed syllables *where they are the second elements of compound words* (thus *–cræft* in *Beo.* 127a, *Grendles gūdcræft*, 'Grendel's war-strength'). Unstressed function words may acquire metrical stress when they're syntactically displaced (*in* in Beo. 19b, *Scedelandum in*, 'in Sweden') but in all the Old English poetry known to me there's *no evidence at all of underlyingly unstressed function words in non-displaced positions being rhythmically promoted so that they bear even relative stress*. It might be objected that 'there's no evidence' applies only to verse ('there's no evidence *in verse*…') but given how closely metres track and stylise the rhythmicity of the vernaculars out of which they're constructed it would be strange to find no trace whatsoever of something like isochrony in Old English verse if isochrony *in* *precisely the form we understand it today* were present in the ancient phonology of the language.

The second argument concerns the harp. Everyone knows that after the construction of Heorot there is rejoicing:

> [...] There was harp-music,
> poet's clear-voiced song.   Who knew, recited,   90
> told the creation   of earth for men,
> said the Almighty   made the landscape,
> eye-restful fields   enfolded by water [...]

Yet the poet's ability to 'sing' (the original has *swutol sang scopes*, 'sweet song of the *scop*') is qualified; the finite verbs that occur in the immediately following half-lines are *sægde*, 'said' and *cwæð*, 'quoth/said'. And it's by no means clear that the *hearpan swēg* and the *swutol sang scopes* are one and the same thing. Lines 89–90 seem to mean not 'there was X, exemplified in Y' but 'there was X [harp-sound] *and there was also* Y [poet's 'song' – or recitation]'. The harp may not have been a constituent part of the recitation at all. In truth, we do not know how the harp was used. It certainly can't be claimed that the harp was used textually, as it were, to generate or reinforce an isochronic performance of the poem. The *Beowulf* poet, therefore, may turn out to be a singer only in the same way Virgil 'sings' the *Aeneid* ('Arms and the man I sing') or that a present-day Poet Laureate may be called a bard.

The foregoing has taken us a long way from definitions of epic and I'm conscious that I've begged several questions. If I don't believe that *Beowulf* is a song then what do I think it is, how do I think its metre was structured and what was I trying to achieve in the translation? Because I need to get back to the vexations of defining epic I'll answer those questions in *How?* below.

In my view, 'epic' describes a literary mode in which a narrative – usually of some length, complexity and diachronic depth, and usually containing both a protagonist and one or more antagonists

– is related to an audience or readership in a medium character-ised by the presence of a set or subset of distinctive, verse-specific conventions and/or constraints. I'm conscious that again this may be an over-simplification, one based on the assumption (which I've tended to make throughout) that epic is a genre somehow 'out there' whose nature we can define taxonomically, as it were. Any genre is likely to become, over time, a hybrid – yet there are also genre boundaries that *Beowulf* doesn't cross. Unlike later Arthuri-an materials, which seem to begin life in poetry and song and are later rendered by Malory into prose, *Beowulf* remains, always and everywhere, a poem, at least until very much later in its textual history – when it becomes a film, a cartoon strip, even a stage play.

The taxonomic definition I've just offered makes the term 'epic' inapplicable both to prose (*Middlemarch* is a novel, not an epic) and to film (*Game of Thrones* is an episodically conducted narra-tive). Of course, we may say that *Game of Thrones* is 'epic', but if we do so, we're not describing its genre nor even its mode, merely those of its characteristics that are reminiscent of those narratives we associate with epic.

Further – and I repeat that I'm aware of its limitations – the same taxonomic definition makes epic distinct from lyric. The diachronic depth of epic may be usefully contrasted with the synchronic sur-faces of lyric. In lyric, the perspective is that of thematic content in-tersecting with all those moments that make up now: lyrics happen in an eternal present tense. 'So long lives this, and this gives life to thee'; Shakespeare's great cry of affirmation, ripped from the most difficult introspection, gains force because what is felt and present, at that moment, will endure through all the moments to come. In Larkin's 'As bad as a mile', preoccupied though the poem appears to be with the historical process of 'failure spreading back up the arm/ Earlier and earlier [...]', the temporal framework is that of the present, indicated in the finite and non-finite verbs of the first three lines: 'Watching the shied core / Striking the basket, skidding across the floor, / Shows less and less of luck, and more and more // Of failure [...]'. Even where a lyric poem is cast into the past tense, the framing – by which I mean the moment of realisation that impels the production and conditions the perception of the poem – obliges readers to understand the emotion of the lyric as being enduringly present. 'Methought,' wrote Milton (past tense), 'I saw my late espoused saint' (Sonnet 23). Yet the effect of Milton's framing in this particular sonnet is to invite the past into the terrible pathos of Now: 'I wak'd, she fled, and day brought back my night' – and the speaker is thereby continually waking, the woman continually fleeing, the poet enduringly blind.

At the risk of restating the already obvious, if action and emotion in a lyric poem are ultimately realised in an eternal present, epics take place in an imaginary history. Naturally, epic poets wish to place themselves and their task in the present ('Arms and the man *I sing*') but the events they describe have already taken place, however the consequences of those events resonate into the present (Virgil again: 'O Muse! the causes and the crimes *relate*,— [present tense: help me tell this story now] / What goddess *was provok'd* [past] and whence her hate; / For what offense the Queen of Heav'n *began* [past] / To persecute so brave, so just a man'). The *Beowulf* poet is more than well aware of these temporal and thematic intersections – so well aware that he chooses to open his poem with them; if *Hwæt* is a monitory call to listen, the listening must take place in the present, yet the first line of *Beowulf* then goes on to link the *Gār-Dena* ('Spear-Danes') with *geār-dagum* (literally, 'yore-days'). Interestingly, he also links himself with his audience: 'we have heard', he says, 'of the might of Danish kings back in the yore-days' – and I am going to tell you about these things (*Hwæt*).

The working definition of epic above also suggests that epic is distinct from romance. Romances – I think here of *Gawain* in the first instance – may centre on the deeds of a protagonist (and/or antagonists), be of diachronic depth and even essay the monstrous, but romance seems to differ from epic in the extent to which the underlying tensions of romantic narratives are, perhaps for the sake of teaching a medieval moral, so often *resolved*: Gawain, after his adventures, does come home, however he may wear a badge of shame; the identity of the green knight is revealed; the story is told. Yet the underlying tensions in *Beowulf* remain largely unresolved.

What are these tensions? They take the form of potential or actual *contrasts* that offer the poem opportunities for thematic development. It's perhaps worth noticing that other, anthropological investigators, most notably Lévi-Strauss (1955), once suggested that something like these contrasts could be compared with the phonemes that make up the underlying sound-structure of a given language, and that therefore they might be called *mythemes*. In begetting one early version of what became known as Structuralism, however, Lévi-Strauss was somewhat coy about whether *mythemes* applied to characters, movements, properties, plot elements of the narrative, intentions or outcomes, and there was no subsequent agreement about what an inventory of *mythemes* might comprise, nor any consensus about how to constrain such an inventory – even if one existed. I also differ from Lévi-Strauss in that I see underlying contrasts not as absolutes but as generative of a scale of narrative possibilities. That is, each putative underlying contrast generates at least three surface terms, and it's the manifestation of these surface terms that seems to be the business of the poet. For example, suppose one underlying contrast is that of human and non-human: [±human]. Now, the *Beowulf* poet might lack many things, but subtlety he does not lack: his poem ranges over the human and all its glorious or baleful attributes (courage and cowardice; gift-giving and greed), the superhuman (Beowulf's miraculous strength), the humanoid (Grendel and his dam) and the non-human (the dragon). Or take a notional underlying contrast such as [±life]. *Beowulf* is as it were absolute for death – one recalls Tolkien writing that the first 3,136 lines of the poem (of a total of 3,182 lines) 'are the prelude to a dirge' (1936, p.33), yet life and death offer no straightforward contrasts in the poem's radically imagined context. [±life] generates third (wounded, dying) and fourth (spiritually dead, exiled among Cain's kin, doomed) categories. Death, too, is seen to have consequences for the living: as the smoke lingers above the pyre on Hronesness, the Geats fear invasion, kidnap and homelessness consequent on a possible, even imminent war with their neighbours, the Swedes. In a brilliant *aperçu*, Heaney likened the scene to something 'from Rwanda or Kosovo' (1999: p.xxi). Similarly, other notional contrasts – rich and poor, earth and sky, land and water, courage and cowardice – offer the *Beowulf* poet not absolute but scalar materials and potential themes out of which his narrative may be built. By the end, the Geats are almost rich, yet the treasure Beowulf has won for his tribe is cursed of old and is burnt on the pyre, therefore they are poor indeed; earth has an under-earth (the dragon's den) and the sky, at the end, is filled by something of and yet not of the earth – a body becoming smoke ('Heofon rēce swealg', line 3155b). Beowulf's barrow is built on a headland, but its meaning is as a beacon for seafarers. Categories shift; meanings are malleable, impermanent; the ironies, like the implied consequences, are tragic. Fate is full forceful.

Some of these properties *Beowulf* shares with the *Aeneid* and the *Odyssey*. I am emphatically not here claiming that the *Beowulf* poet or his predecessors knew of Classical epics, rather suggesting that epic is so useful a literary mode that if it does not yet exist, human cultures will feel obliged to (re)invent it. The *Odyssey*, for instance: it's almost too easy to (mis-)read the poem as a narrative of homecoming, yet Homer was wiser than any of us and knew that whatever 'home' might be, its realities are deeply vulnerable. It doesn't in this sense seem accidental that the *Odyssey* ends not with a resolution in Ithaka, in the great bed made of olive wood, but with the protagonists of the poem in full armour, ready for another campaign, and yet being instructed by the gods to observe the terms of an uneasy peace. Similarly, Hurley and O'Neill suggest that the *Aeneid* 'ends not with any jubilant note, but with Aeneas's slaying of Turnus [...] The downbeat of Virgil's ending reminds us that [...] the major epic poems refuse simply to endorse a propagandist programme' (2012, pp.121–22).

If there are notional contrasts in *Beowulf* – contrasts in whose extended handling the poem may be said to be epic – then epic conventions are found there too. These include statements of *kin and kinship*; *journeys* – often towards points of presumed origin; *encounters with oracles or shamans*; *descents* into an under- or otherworld; *meetings with or invocations of gods* (and in *Beowulf*, with Fate); the testing of physical as well as metaphysical *courage*; *endurance* in the face of overwhelming odds; the challenges posed by *the monstrous and its manifestations*; and a deep but often non-consoling relationship with *the idea and the physical fabric of 'home'*.

That something like these conventions exist can scarcely be doubted by any reader or listener who is remotely familiar with Homer or Virgil. I emphasise again that I am not claiming that the *Beowulf* poet was 'influenced by' Classical models. Rather, he seems to adapt an underlying (even, possibly, a universal) set of storytelling conventions in order to serve his own purpose, which is to make an epic poem. Of these conventions I'd like to lay stress on three, since they were important in the making of the present translation. The first is the significance the poet gives to *kin and kinship*. It was no accident that I chose to open the present work with three family trees, showing respectively the genealogies of the royal houses of Danes, Geats and Swedes. *Beowulf* opens with a statement of the founding of the Danish royal house and with a brief, vivid account of the ship-burial of Scyld Scefing ('Shield Sheafson' in Heaney's translation). Scyld's son (Beow) and grandson (Halfdan) in turn succeeded to the kingdom, and Halfdan fathered four children, among them Hrothgar. Hrothgar's sister, we're told, married Onela, a Swedish king, the son of Ongentheow. Much later in the poem, we're told of Ongentheow's campaign against the Geats and specifically against Hygelac, Beowulf's uncle.

Already the potential for irony – tragic irony – can be found in the very materials and conventions from which the poem is made.

Even the most powerful and most famous of kings slip into the darkness, and no one can say with truth where it is they go. Kingdom may war with kingdom, brother may fight brother. Peace may be patched by the taking of hostages, the payment of *wergild*, or by intermarriage. Yet here also is a world of forcings, abductions, treachery and cowardice.

It's sometimes said that the world of *Beowulf* is 'aristocratic' and 'heroic'. Those terms only make sense to me if they're understood in rather the same way that one might describe Coppola's *The Godfather* (1972) as taking place in an 'aristocratic and heroic' milieu. In both contexts, courtesies and customs are measured against brutality: when they come to Grendel's tarn the Danes look aghast on Aeschere's disembodied head, and meanwhile, in a not too distant elsewhere, '[t]hey shot Sonny on the causeway [...]'. Loyalty can quickly become treachery; courage is known and celebrated the more keenly because cowardice, in the face of overwhelming odds, can seem like sensible self-preservation. Even here, however, in the instantiation of courage and physical strength, there's a potential for tragic irony: Beowulf's courage is sustained by his capacity for endurance and specifically, his massive and terrible grip. Yet in the end, at the end, his physical prowess is a part of what causes his death: as Beowulf attempts to wield Nægling (his sword) on the dragon's second attack, 'wæs sīo hond tō strong' (line 2685):

[...] in need's violence   Nægling shattered.   2680
Beowulf's great sword,   grey-polished, ancient,
weakened in war-play.   It wasn't granted
that swords' edges   had been able, ever,
to help him fight.   His hand – or so I heard –   2685
was too strong; he   overstruck every
blood-hardened blade,   he was none the better for it [...]

This, then, seems to me not so much an imaginative world of aristocracies and kingdoms, of manners whispering in gilt and stone, but one of clans and chieftains – a world of family, in the same sense that *The Godfather* turns on 'the family' and *cosa nostra* (lit. 'our things' or 'our affairs'). It doesn't seem accidental that Hrothgar's first response, when he hears that Beowulf is seeking an audience with him, is to exclaim that (in the present translation), 'I knew him when he was a wean, a boy! His father, his great forebear, was Ecgtheow, to whom Hrethel the Geat gave his daughter in marriage: this man of merit outside is their son, who'll find friends here indeed [...]' – I know him and I know his lineage. He is probably, therefore, *one of us.*

The family or clan is also a place of profound imaginative reassurance. After Beowulf's death what agitates Wiglaf and the immediate clan of the Geats is not so much that the land has been laid waste or the possible presence of another dragon but that catastrophe will befall the tribe in the form of inter-tribal war – 'invasion, kidnap, killing, humiliation' as the text has it (lines 3154–56; Wiglaf's words of lines 3077–78a also invoke the possibility of 'wræc', exile). The clan is weakened, and once news of Beowulf's death spreads then the Swedes, responding both to lord-lack and to blood-feuding smeared resentfully through time, may and probably will attack. 'Home', in the form of a settled imaginative space populated by a clan at peace, shall be no more. So important does this seem that I'll turn to the theme of 'home' below.

A second epic convention is the presence of deities. In *Beowulf*, deities are manifested in both the pagan gods and a Christian God, and the numinous is also present in the form of *wyrd*, usually translated as Fate.

Much ink has been spilled on whether *Beowulf* is brushed or suffused with Christianity. For all the presence of pagan elements – sacrificing to idols, observation of omens, pagan cremations are merely three such mentioned by Klaeber (1950, p.xlviii) – Hrothgar is presented as a Christian king whose counsellors are nevertheless pagans; Beowulf himself, and even though his corpse is burnt in a pagan rite, seems to die a Christian death. Lines 2794ff. (among many other instances) can't really be taken to invoke anything other than a specifically Christian God, even using a formulaic expression ('Wuldur-cyninge' – king of glory) familiar in a Christian context since at least the time of Cædmon – even though the same term probably begins life in secular praise-poetry.

Careful reading of the structure of the poem may help. The passage sometimes called 'Hrothgar's sermon' spans lines 1699–1784 and therefore occupies what is almost the centre of the poem. It is an exploration of the theme of good – in that context, Christian – governance. Acknowledging the temptations to which power is subject, the speech persists in asking not 'what is right conduct?' but 'what, for a ruler, is *the best* conduct?' The best conduct is modulated by acknowledging the presence of God in the imminence of death:

'And so in the end   it also must happen
'that leased life-home,   the flesh, decays,
'is doomed, perishes;   another prince succeeds,   1755
'one who guiltlessly   gives out treasures,
'fair, ancient wealth,   and fears no terrors.
'Guard against such hate-lashing,   honoured Beowulf
'and best of men.   Choose the better road – to
'eternal gains.   Give pride no place,   1760
'my beloved champion.   It shall linger a while,
'the glory of your power,   but presently it shall be
'that sickness or the sword   shall unseat your strength,
'or the flames' embrace,   or the flood's whelming,
'or the blade in spite,   or the spear in flight,   1765
'or the horror of age,   or the once-keen eyes
'failing, dim-shadowed;   and soon it shall be due
'to you, dear warrior: death shall overpower you.

'Give pride no place'... Yet as soon as we, the audience, are told that pride should be given no place, it is given a place. The injunction can be analogised with telling someone not to think of elephants. And Beowulf is undoubtedly prideful. In order to fight the dragon he dons armour – a concession to fire and circumstance – but says explicitly that the contest will be 'a measure of my strength against monstrousness, my customary gift of great courage' (lines 2534–35). By this time, we know – and Beowulf knows – that he is old. His sword buckles; his chosen men have fled and their word of honour – the code – has been broken; it is, finally, *wyrd* that will decide on the outcome of Beowulf's God-granted free will. I do not think I will be alone if I read Wiglaf's subsequent words (given below in the present translation) as a mixture of bafflement and criticism:

'If one man's wilful,   many others must
'endure exile.   This has befallen us.
'By no counsel   or claim could we advise
'our beloved chieftain,   our land's warden,   3080
'not to go to meet   the gold-guardian
'but to let him lie   where he'd lived so long,
'waiting in his earth-halls   until the world ended.
'He held to his high purpose,   and the hoard's open,
'gifted so grimly...'

In the translation I emphasised lines 3077–78a simply because they have the force of a gnomic expression. The modal 'must', for example, is a verb that here has epistemic force because the general proposition is evidenced by Beowulf's wilfulness in the face of counsel and his rashness in the face of age. Certainly, much is made of the cowardice of his companions, the battle-shirkers, but it's hard not to avoid the conclusion that Beowulf dies in his pride – rather as Byrhtnoth, in *Maldon*, is cut down by heathens at the very moment that he is laughing and giving thanks to God. Yet what hero is not hubristic? Beowulf dies as a hero, and the encomium on his virtues that concludes the poem cannot be taken to be disingenuous. The tragedy is that despite his epic heroism, the world he sought to protect – the context of home and of tribe – is now in danger of annihilation. There will merely be a barrow on a headland, and blood blooming in rain-water, and the smell of smoke on the wind. There has been no right choosing, because there could not be. Worlds have passed or are passing away. Fate is full forceful.

A third epic convention is the relationship of its characters with the idea of 'home'. Clearly, in calling the exploration of the idea of home an 'epic convention' I have in mind poems such as the *Odyssey* (though I stress again that the *Odyssey* should not be misread purely as a narrative of homecoming), but an interest in 'home' also permeates the *Iliad*, where characters experience home-sickness, and the *Aeneid*, where the protagonist is forced to flee one home in order eventually to found another.

'Home' is of course, and possibly primarily, a physical fabric. It doesn't seem coincidental that the incursions of Grendel and his dam, and Beowulf's fight with Grendel, literally shake Heorot's walls and floor:

> Hall-timbers dinned.   Among the Danes there,
> each of the men who   manned the stronghold,
> there was desperate terror.   Tearing anger
> filled both fighters;   the frame of the hall   770
> resounded – miraculous   that its rafters stood
> fury's combat,   that it didn't fall to earth,
> such a fair structure;   but it was strengthened
> inside and out   with iron shackles
> forged skillfully.   (Yet its furnishings,   775
> gathered mead-benches   with their gold cladding,
> battered from their bases   while the bale played out –
> or so I've heard rumoured.)   Could they ever have reckoned,
> the Scylding *witan*   with their wise counsels,
> that their splendid hall,   hung with antlers,   780
> could threaten to shatter,   be shaken by cunning –
> unless fire swallowed it?

– nor that Grendel's fearsome hand is set on Heorot's roof; nor that after the slaying of his dam, Grendel's head is brought back to Heorot and dragged in to the hall. As a physical space, too, Heorot is richly decorated, and its ornate furnishings contrast with the debris in the mere (and later in the poem, and implicitly, with the tarnished silver and rusted iron of the Worm's hoard).

More structurally, 'home' in *Beowulf* seems to work on two dimensions, the one psychological, the other geographic. The geographic position of the Danish court, a court eventually located in Heorot, is central: as early as line 9, tribes situated around and 'across the swan-road' (the sea) from the Danes are described in a telling metaphor as 'ymb-sittend', literally 'around-sitting'. As Heorot is built, treasures are ordered brought to it from kingdoms 'geond þisne middan-geard' (throughout this middle-earth, line 75); it's hard to resist the temptation to read Heorot as lying in this part of the poem like the hub in a political and cultural wheel. That temptation is strengthened when one reads that Heorot, long associated with Lejre (in present-day Zealand, Denmark), shed its light over the lands around it (line 311 – Alexander's translation goes further and tells how 'its radiance lighted the lands of the world'). Heorot, that is, seems to participate in part of the myth of its own creation: it is 'wlite-beorht' (fair to look on, see also line 93); it towers ('Sele hlī-fade', line 81b) – a source of wonder, gift-giving, and radiant light. For its glorious clan chief, as for his kin and court, it is home.

The psychological dimension of 'home' is no less important. In a provocative and useful paper from 2002, the clinical psychologist Renos Papadopoulos explores concepts of 'home' as those might pertain to the traumatic situations of refugees and other displaced persons. Calling 'home' a 'fundamental notion' of humanity', he first cites the OED's definition of home:

[a] place, region or state to which one properly belongs, in which one's affections centre, or where one finds refuge, rest or satisfaction' (OED, cited in Papadopoulos 2002 p.2)

and goes on to suggest that most homes:

> provide some kind of continuity that enables co-existence between many opposites: love and discord, distance and proximity, joys and sorrows, hopes and disappointments, flexibility and obstinacy, envy and magnanimity, rivalry and collaboration, loyalty and betrayal, enmity and friendship, similarities and differences [...]
>
> [...] Homes can provide that deep and fundamental sense of space where all these opposites and contradictions can be contained and held together. Inevitably, this develops a sense of security (Papadopoulos 2002, p.6)

That sense of security, he suggests, may be called *onto-ecological settledness* – an ontological concept because it is essentially comparative and evaluative, i.e. one's home at a given moment may be psychologically compared with other possible homes. And accordingly, homecoming may be described not merely as a geographically retrogressive action but as the *re-establishment of connection* with place, kin, or tribe; further, the non-pathological but nevertheless psychologically potent condition of *homesickness* may be described as 'nostalgic disorientation'.

In some Old English poetry, 'home' is co-opted for specifically Christian purposes, perhaps most overtly in the conclusion to the elegy 'The Wanderer':

> All struggles, all is spent   on the span of earth:
> 'world turns, fractious;   fate-stroke is fickle.
> 'Property vanishes;   patron vanishes;
> 'mankind vanishes;   kindred... All vanish.
> 'All made in time   was mortal, useless.'
> *So he spoke, runing   at wisdom's rim.*
> Yet may good fall to one   who guards his faith rightly,
>   whose grief remains silent;
> who renders remedy   for bitterness of mind,

<blockquote>
for the wreckage of hope;
whose conduct is courage.   Care-worn, mind-torn,
may his grace be mercy,
a hope of heaven,   that offers to all
a home, haven.
[my translation]
</blockquote>

The *Beowulf* poet, of course, eschews such explicitly Christian conclusions. As heaven swallows the smoke from Beowulf's funeral pyre, meanings and contrasts are suspended, the future is unknown, what lasts are only the certain uncertainties of a story of blood and renown. Fate is full forceful.

How tempting it must have been for this poet to have written a more specifically Christian epic, one in which the forces of Satanic darkness – Cain's kin, the Lost – were pitted against the brilliant and consoling shields of the Saved. It is quite true that the poet observes his imaginative world from a Christian, humane and a highly literate perspective, but that serves to give added pathos to his story and his vision. And as Tolkien rightly stated, the dragon of *Beowulf* may be a personification of 'malice, greed, destruction (the evil side of heroic life)' (p.17) but nevertheless the underlying symbolism never quite becomes allegory. Beowulf never brandishes the Sword of Heavenly Justice; his retainers never raise the Banners of Righteousness. Had they done so, *Beowulf* would have been a different poem – and very much less of one.

In my own readings of the poem, 'home' played an increasingly important role. At first, I suppose I understood the poem linearly and episodically – Scyld's funeral; the coming of Grendel; arrival of Beowulf at Heorot; swimming match with Breca; fight with Grendel and so on – as if *Beowulf* was, rather like the *Kalevala*, a more or less (and usually less) unified collection of folk tales, themed around monster-slaying. This was Ker's view (*The Dark Ages*, 1904): the story, carried in 'three chief episodes' is (he wrote) 'too simple'. The history of the *Beowulf* manuscript, too – specifically the Nowell Codex, in which the poem is preserved – suggest that time and chance somewhat casually bound *Beowulf* together with a work of prose, 'The Wonders of the East', because their common theme was marvels, monsters and the miraculous. Yet the more I thought about 'home' during the making of the present translation, the less episodic and fantastic did *Beowulf* seem to become. To be clear, the poem now seems to me to include a penetrating examination of all that 'home' can mean – and embodies almost all conceivable threats to that sense of 'onto-ecological settledness' imaginable. In this imaginative world, 'home' can be imagined:

(i) as **genealogy**
The peaceful transition from leader to leader; the persistence of a royal family, each of whose kings generates and distributes wealth fairly;

(ii) as **geography**
Psychological centrality of home-space; the potential for change occupying the periphery;

(iii) as **nation (clan, tribe)**
Inheriting a settled system of laws and local customs; where family names are recognised and social values understood.

In exploring the centrality of 'home' to *Beowulf* it should not be understood, of course, that Hrothgar's or Beowulf's retainers were home-bodies, fond of a spot of gardening or cooking. Nor should a phrase such as 'distributes wealth fairly' (above) be understood to imply that this was a democratic society. It was not: it was a slave society. What counted was blood, or gold, or that equally precious commodity, a good name. There might have been counsel, but there were no votes.

I have already touched above on themes such as kin and kinship. Embedded in royal genealogies, however, even claims of kin and kinship may be disruptive. The founder of the Scylding dynasty arrives in Denmark from who-knows-where; Beowulf is himself adopted into the Geat royal house; and Beowulf has no blood suc- cessor. Within any royal genealogy, too, is the potential for treach- ery or civil war – brother may fight brother, kings may go to the bad – and if peace between clans is sealed by bride-gift, that too may generate war. Further, if one of the duties of a good king is gift-giving (something the poet emphasises as early as line 20) then strategic generosity, too, can be destabilised by covetousness, as in the tale of Heremod:

'Heremod was not so
'for Ecgwel's sons,   the Scyldings of old.   1710
'He didn't grow to joy,   but to great slaughter,
'death and destruction   of the Danish tribe.
'His closest friends   he killed while they ate.
'He was enraged, brooding.   At last he bent alone,
'that once-famous figure,   from the fair world's joys,   1715
'although Almighty God   in merit and power
'had advanced him far –   further in fact than
'all other men.   Yet in his mind there spawned
'some blood-hunger.   He blessed no Dane
'with due ring-giving.   Dream-darkened he   1720
'lived, lashed by spirit –   a lingering trouble
'to his tribe for years.   Be taught by that:
'understand true goodness!   This tale I tell
'wintered in wisdom.

From this perspective, too, Grendel and his dam are both horrify- ing and tragic. Their great progenitor was Cain:

From him are descended   all sin's offspring –
the monsters, the elves,   orc-corpses, carrion –
those misbegotten,   who contended with God

on time's causeway   until His requital...
(lines 111–14)

And Grendel, too, is ironically described as a ruler:

> So Grendel ruled,   an inglorious
> one among many.   It stood empty at night   145
> at last, the hall.   Those years were long:
> their troubles he endured   for twelve winters,
> the Scyldings' lord –   lost in miseries,
> the country of sorrows

He and his kin (his dam) live peripherally to Heorot – Grendel is described, before his first attack, as waiting enraged in darkness – and he subverts all laws and social customs:

> [...] Truce he
> couldn't accept from   any son of the Danes,   155
> wouldn't cease from malice   or settle for terms;
> of the company, none   could expect compensation
> for slain kinsmen   at their slayer's hands.

'Compensation' means the system of *wergild* (literally, 'man-price'), by which restitution could be made to the family of a murdered victim by the perpetrator. (The alternative to such payment was blood revenge.) Line 157 is yet another tragic foreshadowing, of the story of Geatish king Hrethel, who dies of grief after his eldest son, Herebeald, is accidentally killed by his younger brother, Hæthcyn. How, in that context, could wergild be paid? To whom? By whom? And how could any other form of blood revenge be contemplated? And here again the *Beowulf* poet structurally emphasises *consequences*: the consequences of that accidentally fateful arrow include not only Hrethel's death but subsequent tribal war between Geats and Swedes.

Grendel and his dam, therefore, participate in but are radically destabilising of imaginative concepts of 'home'. They even live in a different medium. If I may revert briefly to the system of structural contrasts to which I earlier alluded, then if Heorot is constructed centrally within the imaginative world of the poem, and decorated with the gifts of 'many people of middle-earth' (lines 74–75), then it is unambiguously [+earth]. Grendel is described as occupying 'wastelands, margins [...] the monstrous marsh' (lines 103–04) – a place that is both earth and water [±earth]. And Grendel's dam, like Grendel himself, ultimately issues from and returns to a mere, a medium that is unambiguously [-earth] – a mere, moreover, whose subterranean depths are adorned by a different kind of 'tribute', by bones and swords (line 1557).

If Grendel and his dam, as human+oid (and as exiles who live in a state of home+less+ness) participate in and legitimise 'home' by their very subversion of concepts of genealogy, geography and nation, the dragon participates in and legitimises nothing. It has no genealogy or kin, but has slept for at least three hundred years; its geography is either air (line 2871) or under-earth (the barrow, line 2212); it has no fixed territory but is a 'night-flyer [...] a seeker out of smouldering barrows' (line 2272); it knows no nation, laws or noble customs. Yet its meaning within the poem is clearly not merely to subvert but to destroy 'home'.

Beowulf, by then king of the Geats, is destroyed by the dragon. There is no peaceful transition of the kingship to an heir, and Beowulf specifically remarks at the end of his life that he would bequeath his battle-gear 'to a son [...] if I'd been granted such an inheritor' (lines 2729–30). Further, the treasure Beowulf has won for his people is cursed, and therefore unusable and valueless.

If the dragon destroys 'home' as genealogy, it also destroys 'home' as geography. Its rage of covetousness torches the bright farmsteads of the Geatish nation and firelight burns in eyes everywhere (lines 2312–14); even Beowulf's own throne-room is torched (lines 2325–26). The dragon's destructive power also extends to the coastline (line 2335).

And the dragon destroys 'home' as nation. I don't think it's insignificant that the concern expressed by Wiglaf after Beowulf's death is largely focussed on the threat to the Geat people of exile, of war and consequent homelessness:

'And that is the feud –   fierce enmity,
'unfinished slaughter –   I sorrow about,   3000
'which will cause the tribe   of Swedes to attack
'as soon as they've heard   that our high lord lies
'with his life taken,   who always protected
'our land and assets   against all enemies [...]

'[...] No part of the treasure,   3010
'the massive hoard,   shall remain unmelted:
'that countless gold,   so cruelly bought,
'and numberless rings,   are now at the last
'paid for with his passage.   The pyre will eat,
'flame enfold them: no fighter shall wear   3015
'treasures as tokens,   no attractive girl
'have a ring-necklace   resting on her shoulders.
'Lost, pain-stricken,   deprived of the gold,
'often they'll wander   down exile's ways
'now their leader is dead   and his laughter, pleasure   3020
'and happiness doomed.   Many a dawn-cold spear,
'therefore, shall be wrapped   in fighters' fists,
'raised and brandished;   it's not the ringing harp
'that shall wake warriors   but the war-glutted raven
'busy over corpses,   his baleful voice   3025
'telling the eagle   how avidly he choked
'as he and the wolf   ate the war-offal.'

The same concern is echoed by the woman who sings Beowulf's death-lay as his corpse becomes flame. Her song:

[...] expressed

her fear that time   would fill with terror –
vicious invasion,   vile kidnap, killing,
humiliation
  [lines 3152–55]

A nation – a home well and justly ruled by Beowulf for fifty years –
has become a kingdom of blackened bones. There's only the smell
of fire on the wind. Heaven has swallowed the smoke. Fate is full
forceful.

I have never yet read a critical account of *Beowulf* that has engaged with the whole poem in precisely these terms – which is not
to claim that the present foray is correct, or even that it's along the
right lines. I found Marijane Osborn's recent work on the material
culture of *Beowulf* of great interest (in eds. Chickering et al. 2014,
p.189ff.), and I am also taken with the post-colonial reading of
Beowulf sketched by Johnston (in the same 2014 volume), in which
Grendel's identity may be read as that of 'the Danes' excluded Other' (p.234) and Beowulf's descent into the mere as an analogue of
Marlow's expedition into the heart of darkness (p.237). Yet perhaps the closest view to my own is that of Kathryn Hume (1975)
who, posing the question 'What is *Beowulf* about?', explores the
proposition that the 'controlling theme' of the poem is 'threats to
social order' (p.5). The poem's structure, she argues, can be seen as
a 'sequence of these threats, each embodied in a suitable monster'
(p.6). Hume's conception of social order lies close to my own no-
tions concerning *Beowulf*'s preoccupation with good governance
and, like Hume, I read (and have translated) the actions of the three
antagonists in the poem, as well as what used to be called the historical 'digressions', as related to that overarching theme. That is, I
do not think that the 'digressive' materials – the accounts of Finn,
Ingeld, the Heathobard feud, the Swedish wars – are actually digressive: each sheds light on how governance can be threatened and
how order can be maintained. I also agree, and profoundly, with
Hume that if 'the digressions' *were* digressions then one would

expect the poem to read as more episodic and less unified. And I agree with Hume's critical instincts about the epic worlds of both *Beowulf* and the later *Morte*:

> Malory and the *Beowulf*-poet seem to me startlingly similar in method. Neither was recreating a genuine past; nor were they seeking mythical golden ages. Rather, they each took a system of values which was the theoretical ideal reflected in ruling class entertainment but not put into practice – the heroic and the chivalric codes of behavior. They created 'past' worlds by giving life to these theories, and then tried to understand the forces which could have caused such societies to fail, or to degenerate to what they themselves lived in. [p.26]

Coupling *Beowulf* with the *Morte* brings me back to the question with which I began this Afterword: What kind of a poem is *Beowulf*? For all the reasons I've explored, I believe *Beowulf* is an epic whose central theme is good governance. Its protagonist is Beowulf; its antagonists are the monsters, each of whom poses a different sort of threat to the social order described in the poem. The poem utilises both historical and imaginative materials to explore its central theme, and is alert throughout to the consequences of the actions of all its characters. An important and recurrent sub-theme is that of 'home': as well as exploring how governance can be good the poem also explores how 'home' – defined here as onto-ecological settledness – might be constructed and how it can be destroyed. The imaginative milieu of *Beowulf* is heroic, deeply legalistic and tribal. One of its central modes – using the term mode to mean 'that which both generates and modulates the actions described in the poem' – is irony. So pervasive is this irony that as all contrasts and modulations are suspended at the end of the poem we experience the poem not only as an epic, but as a tragic epic.

I'd add one further thing. If *Beowulf* is an epic then, like other epics, its resonances are contemporary. Many of us experience homesickness or conversely, feel the joy (or dislocation) of home-coming. We have an idea of what justice, fairness and good governance might entail. Uncomfortably, too, we might be aware of destructive forces in ourselves – pride, covetousness, depression, even the capacity for self-interest and treachery – and it's probably useful for any reader to be reminded of and to participate in an imaginative reality in which actions have consequences. The poet and his poem ranges over these materials. This is not a vanished world, but a world of vanishings in which to be mortal is also to be tragically unconsoled. Unlike the homilist or the allegorist, the poet of *Beowulf* looks at that truth and is unflinching. A world is passing away. Yet that world is also this one, sited in the transient *Here* in which we read. *Hear from yesterday.*

Strangely, too, and despite the fact that the events of the poem take place in Denmark and southern Sweden, *Beowulf* can in some ways be read as the nearest thing the English language has to a national epic, one which explores and sums the certain uncertainties of kindness and courage and embodies both vitally in its mortal protagonist.

So politically febrile are these times that I would urge any reader to understand the phrase 'national epic' in the full context of the last sentence. I do not mean that *Beowulf* is somehow jingoistic – few poems could be less so – and nor do I mean that the poem could be appropriated as, for example, a happy hunting-ground for mottos that might serve the more foolish of contemporary English political parties. It's also wise to remember that the action of *Beowulf* doesn't take place in England: Hrothgar's scout doesn't patrol the cliffs of Dover. What I do affirm, however, is that this poem is *the nearest thing the English language has* to a national epic. That is, the lexicon, the morphology and the metricality of the poem stand in a fairly similar relationship – it is essentially one of stylisation – to the English language as some (though not all) other epics stand in relation to the vernaculars in which they are composed. It may not be altogether fanciful to think that what Virgil's hexameters were to Augustan Rome the *Beowulf* poet's half-lines could have been to Winchester or York. Furthermore, and particularly if one ascribes a later rather than an earlier date to the process, when the story materials of *Beowulf* were finally assembled into their present (or something like their present) epic structure, then that occurred when English people could probably, and for the first time, think of themselves as English. From blood and bitter sword-play, from radical doubt, from centuries of migration and settlement, even from (in response to) the sails of the longships appearing so terrifyingly off the Northumbrian coast, England had developed religious and secular laws, the greatest vernacular literature in Europe and crucially, literacy. *Beowulf*, though its story is set in an earlier, largely pagan time, provides one way of understanding how the doom of a mortal protagonist may be judged in his relationship with kin and home, with tribe and by extension, with nation. After Finnsburh, Hildeburh is taken home to what is already called Denmark; Beowulf's body is burnt in Geatland, on Hronesness, but as the flames crackle and heaven swallows the smoke he also dies back into the English language from which his poem was made.

HOW?

In the opening section of this Afterword I mentioned a tent in Greenland. It was 2004, I had just left (as I then thought) full-time academic life, I was fishing and constructing some feature articles for the angling press. It was a strenuous trip and included several nights spent alone, camping in remote parts of the country. As a companion I'd taken along my old student text of *Beowulf* – a battered Wrenn/Bolton edition (1973). The paperback was slightly lighter to carry in the rucksack than the great Klaeber edition, and was replete with my own and others' pencil or biro annotations. I read in the long, late summer dusks, or by torchlight. Sometimes, there was no other human presence within a hundred square miles – only something occasionally moving in the darkness, peripheral to the pitiful flare of light around the tent.

My only injunction to myself was to read *Beowulf* as a poem. For many years previously, and like many other philologists, I'd tended to use *Beowulf* primarily as a quarry for interesting linguistic specimens – specimens of particular spellings yielding dialectal evidence; specimens of recalcitrant half-lines; specimens of syntax. I'd written a PhD thesis, after all, largely on Old English verse form and metrics (1988, particularly Vol. II), and there, *Beowulf* loomed large as a text providing critical evidence to an enquiring philologist. Yet in 2004, there in the undistracted light of the Arctic, I wasn't too interested in evidence. I simply wanted to read for pleasure, and in so doing, perhaps join myself up with a younger, less inauthentic self, while remaining fully aware that no such thing as an 'authentic self' existed. Perhaps, after all, the act of re-reading *Beowulf* was merely a nostalgic gesture.

Perhaps. Yet much that was new began there, in solitariness. I found that I couldn't, after all, altogether discard the philologist in me, and the act of re-reading *Beowulf* brought to mind all those other Old English poems I'd once studied, and even occasionally taught, particularly those texts participating in or evincing something of what I still then thought of as 'the heroic': *The Battle of Maldon*, for example, written in or just after 991. Yet thinking of *Maldon* also made me think of the endlessly problematic dating of *Beowulf*. If *Maldon* was commissioned from an antiquarian, could it have been that this earnest pasticheur also knew *Beowulf*? Or did he reach back into the stock diction and formulas of 'the heroic'? Similarly, re-reading some of the more elegiac passages in *Beowulf* made me wish to return to some of the great Old English elegies and their theme of uncertainly redeemed loneliness. There seemed to me to be a fundamental kinship between an emotionally paralysed King Hrethel, grieving his son, and the disconsolation described in 'The Wanderer':

Terrible, it will be terrible   for the true-sighted
when all the world's riches   are wrecked by time –
just as now, today,   on the doomed world's crust
old walls stand awry   and are wind-stricken,
buildings are snow-swept,   snecked by ice-candles.
Vanished are the wine-halls;   winner and victim
lie deprived of prayer.   Pride? Extinguished:
mounds of corpses.   Combat took some,
fared them further: this one the storm-fowl carried
over ocean's deep;   to this one death was dealt
by grinning hoar-wolf;   and this one... Gallow-faced he
graved his gold-friend   in the gaunt earth's depth
   [translation mine; adapted from 'The Wanderer', *Old English
Poems and Riddles*, 2008, line 73ff.]

Yet Hrethel's sorrow is particularised within a legal framework: no *wergild* can be paid for dead Herebeald, since he was slain accidentally by his younger brother, Hæthcyn. The tragic irony only intensifies the old man's grief: he dies in an agony of spirit, whereas 'The Wanderer' offers a specifically Christian consolation (that is, a 'home') to the sick at heart.

... Yet there I was, reading in a crepuscular Arctic, already doing something I was willing myself not to do: being critical, comparative, even evaluative. At some point I began to ask myself how I could embody some of the questions I was beginning to ask about *Beowulf* and other Old English poems in a series of translations. I stress that I had no ambition and no programme.

No ambition, no programme, no qualifications as a translator, no deadline and no contract... When I returned home, and partly as an experiment, I tried to translate some shorter Old English poems. I revisited riddles I'd first studied as an undergraduate, trying to construct present-day analogues for the metrical structures I found in the original texts. That was important, because I'd always believed that *how* something was said was part of *what* was said. I found (i) that to make some of the originals run at all in present-day English it was necessary to make a much freer use of the possibilities of enjambment than would ever have been possible in Old English; (ii) that finding the right balance between Romance and Germanic diction was, for me, an almost insuperable problem; (iii) that the syntax and metrics of the originals seemed – to borrow a phrase of Tolkien's – 'more like masonry than music' (1936, p.31).

At that stage, I could after a fashion form a translation that was reminiscent of the aural architecture of the originals. The very short texts – the riddles – seemed to work fairly well, if only because there was insufficient ambit for me to make too many mistakes; the draft translations of the elegies seemed imperfect, but others seemed to find them passable, if only as pastiches; the rhythmical prose passage from Wulfstan – a howl of exasperation at the English – seemed to capture *something* of the liveliness of the archbishop's fury. These texts I included in an ever-expanding typescript. It was only at a later stage, in 2006, that I thought about turning the typescript into a small book that might prove attractive to those coming to these texts for the first time. Yet such a book, I reckoned, would feel incomplete if I didn't include at least some passages from *Beowulf*.

It was a blunder, to try to include passages from *Beowulf* in what was eventually published as *Old English Poems and Riddles*. I'll be frank: my talents, such as they are, weren't then up to the task. I doubt they are altogether up to it now, but then again... Well, no. Back then, there were some lines, or some gatherings of lines, that I could get to work readably – some of them even lie, scrutinised but unchanged, in the present translation – but elsewhere I felt obliged to overuse run-on half-lines simply to make recognisable metrical patterns; if I tried to match the originating poet's skill with innovative compounds I was bound to fail; in some thematically complex passages – notably those passages surrounding the finding of the hoard – I marred (even mangled) meanings by trying too hard to disambiguate who precisely was doing what to whom; and the diction seems driven more by the needs of metre than by appropriacy. Looking back – and I have, heaven knows, looked back – there are some things I wouldn't change and have not changed, but the earlier attempt at translating even short passages from *Beowulf* was, really, a false start. I well remember giving a copy of *Old English Poems and Riddles* to a colleague. A few weeks later he approached me smilingly in a corridor. 'Thanks so much for the book, Chris,' he said. 'Your work on *Beowulf*, now...' There was a pause in which I braced myself to receive the shower of compliments that was surely coming. 'These are,' he said slowly, 'very much a *metrist's* translations...'

I had never before been damned with such faint praise. Elsewhere, *Old English Poems and Riddles* received some kind reviews, but also attracted less favourable notices. Everything the critics said was true, I thought, and clearly, I needed time to think again. Yet life moves swiftly, the period between 2009–2012 was unusually busy, and even then, having done what little I could with the poem, I had no thought of returning to *Beowulf*. The work lay unfinished. I had done my best, but it had been a poor best and there was no more time to do better.

When Monika and I moved to Essex in 2013 I began to wonder again whether I could or should try to complete the abandoned work. I sketched some of the problems I was then confronting – chiefly, how to translate the monstrous – to a kind audience at a departmental research seminar (2014). At the end of the session someone asked when I expected to finish the draft. 'It'll be at least another three years,' I said, failing to add that the putative three years might well come to mean 'at no time in the remotely foreseeable future'. Nevertheless, and however sporadically, I did keep returning to the translation, working piecemeal, forever unconvinced.

So many and so apparently irremediable were the deficiencies of my false start, and so formidable the challenges of revising it and of then undertaking a full translation, that I doubt I would ever have completed the present work had it not been for a diagnosis of a type of leukaemia, treatment for which kept me away from university work in the period spanning the winter and early spring of 2015–16. For a while, it was impossible to concentrate; anaemia can be brutal when it comes to wiping out the extended ability to focus. For many weeks, it was difficult to read for more than five minutes; it was almost impossible to write anything other than the shortest emails. It's true that I was given outstanding medical advice that combined the kind and the stern in equal measure: *take it easy* seemed to be everyone's cry. Yet I was too unimaginative to take 'it' – whatever it was – easy. At first, unable to read or write, I fretted. I tried pottering about in the garden in the December rain, but I was too weak even to potter. I tried writing short poems and the results were shocking. I tried to read novels I'd put off forever and couldn't get through more than a paragraph, even having resorted to large font on an electronic reading device. I tried looking on the internet at fishing tackle I couldn't afford but became blurry-eyed and resentful. I fretted some more, watching from a reclining chair as winter's sick light fell over the Colne valley. And of course, there was always daytime TV.

I can imagine that many people enjoy daytime TV. One can peer at other people buying or failing to buy houses; there are programmes about antiques, or garden design; there are talk shows, and regular news bulletins, and occasionally, there are working dogs and something to do with vegetables.

After watching daytime TV for a couple of mornings I decided instead to try and translate the opening three lines of *Beowulf*. It's strange, how this poem sets translators one of the most formidable challenges in literature in its first three lines. From sheer cowardice I'd put off revisiting this opening after a failed (and unpublished) first attempt from several years before. Here's that attempt:

Now then. On the ness of time,   news: of Spear-Danes
vanished in years'-dark,   valiant princes,
victories and vanity,   violence and endurance
  [abandoned draft]

It was Grevel Lindop – dear, astute, kind Grevel – who had pointed out, against all my protestations, that 'Now then' made the *Beowulf* poet sound like some sort of demented Anglo-Saxon policeman. And, even setting aside the obtrusive presence of those riotously alliterating /v/ phonemes, even I could hear that 'victories and vanity, violence…' belonged both to the wrong register (= diction too Latinate) and promised the listener what another kind reader, Jeremy Solnick, called a 'sword-and-sorcery epic'. Now (or even 'Now then'), *Beowulf* may be many things, but it doesn't belong comfortably, or even at all, in a sword-and-sorcery genre. And so, as an alternative to watching daytime TV, mid-way through treatment for leukaemia, I began to fiddle with *Beowulf*. By that time, as I've confessed above, I had already completed, or abandoned, a draft translation of some passages, including the poem's final lines, so I didn't come to the fiddling cold, as it were. It was more in the character of a return to the almost impossible.

I did something else, too, while I was recovering and fiddling. Two years earlier I'd been working with a class of second-year writing students on an exercise that involved creating a synoptic narrative. I found this exercise first in the pages of Hazel Smith's *The Writing Experiment* (2005), where the author describes working with a form of synoptic novel (p.194ff.). Since my class were researching and writing in different kinds of narrative form I wondered whether we could work together on something like a 'synoptic epic' – an epic radically compressed into ten lines. To achieve the compression, formal characteristics of (Classical) epics – such as invocations of the Muse, kinship statements, presence of a protagonist, themes of governance – would have to be first identified and then deployed, with the caution that each synoptic epic should contain *at least three* such characteristics. Because I don't set my students writing exercises I can't or won't do myself, I tried to explore the sort of thing I thought I wanted. The result was a poem which, in the original typescript, was exactly ten lines long:

They were somebody's, after all. Tell it? I'll try, but they're all gone, the ones who could. And who remembers Paris now? The cell, the trial, the flashguns. #helen meeja lyres smashed *innocent face*. No one doubted he'd had it hard, then they forgot him and he disappeared. When the rumours came from Turkey some were thinking of the recession and others were out of time. The cell had been turned into one of those chrome places that do coffee, the starlings were nesting in decades'-old human hair and the Simois was a greasy open pipe. He walked through Arrivals looking tanned and fit and the girl was still with him. By then, the chief witness was...unreliable. They'd made a fortune – in poppies. They say he went back to his first wife. We didn't hear he'd died until years later. The other girl bought a farm, somewhere in Norfolk I think. She was found hanged.

Then I wrote another:

Stood on the shore of the great salt rivers. A mammoth carcase sang in the wind. The problem was floods and what to do with the corpses. Villages no-one had heard of floated past towards Doggerland. Discovered fire when fen became coal, and flint was useful, also for building. Opened the anthology and it was empty. Blamed the others and tried to plug in the lights but there was no electricity. Earth talked and it wasn't reassuring. Wives farrowed. That passed the time. There were no messages and the sky was lonely. By then it was an issue: how to converse with tundra that had become tideline. Tried to trade it away for a piece of amber but settled for a bone. Pierced it with the tongue of a buckle. That night the ambient gods spoke through a hollowed pipe while the weather hurled from the north-west. Death was a flute in a femur. Children danced. A lake appeared, and giraffes. Music became settlements.

And because by this time, several weeks into chemotherapy, I was returning to *Beowulf* and failing to watch daytime TV or take it easy, another:

Time's wreckage: ten haunches, swung in the smoke-house. Eadgyth, stoop-shouldered, at work flensing the Testaments. (She was Gudric's woman, Morcar's brother's wife: a good breeder.) Across the courtyard, flayed from its last ditch, a boar, dung-barrowed. Antlers awry on lintels, mead-cups still moist, tables over-turned. Stale air in hall, tainted with taken breath. They went out early to look at the floods. No prayer has been proof against the rain. Winter planting is wasted and the strangers have sent a great ship-army out of the North. Eadric throttled a dog that maimed a child. Godwy was set adrift in a boat without oars. They say the king is penitent, has decreed psalm-books and a church, but no-one comes and his promises are a box of rusty hinges. Dusk falls in on its swart shroud, owls fly shrieking at the edge of the world and all eyes watch for what claw might crack, what down murk move.

As these synoptic epics continued to come, I realised far too belatedly not only that these structures were allowing me to explore what writing, reading and listening to 'epic' might involve, but also that each of the new pieces was themed around death. The presence of death in the poems shouldn't be taken to mean that somehow these new pieces emerged directly from cancer, chemotherapy and a personal encounter with the promise of extinction, but that they, like their models, were formed in a mode of verbal art that, to re-use Hurley and O'Neill's happy phrase, 'consorts with ironic dust' (2012, p.120).

As I worked on the synoptic epics I was also doing rather more than fiddling with the *Beowulf* translation. The two projects began to speak to one another: the more I was embodying what I was learning about epic in the synoptic epics, the less satisfied I became with my earlier attempts to translate bits of *Beowulf*, and the readier I became to return to the original and begin again what Eliot in 'East Coker' (1940) called 'the intolerable wrestle / With words and meanings'. The more I learned from working with *Beowulf* about how epic themes were manifested in that poem, the more eager I became to explore other epic themes in the synoptic texts.

As the chemotherapy proceeded into its third month I found I could translate possibly up to eight lines of *Beowulf* in a day. As a third month turned into a fourth I was able to translate up to around twenty lines a day, very rarely more. I revised what I had already done, in the false start of 2005–8, as thoroughly as I could, particularly the account of the discovery of the hoard, and always revised the previous day's efforts before proceeding with any new group of lines. Perhaps perversely, the opening three lines of *Beowulf* proved resistant to many attempts to translate them satisfactorily, and it was only quite late in the renewed drafting process that I revised the umpteenth attempt at the opening to:

Hear from yesterday,   from the yore-days,
of the Spear-Danes

It was Jeremy Solnick who suggested the initial half-line, and I'm delighted to acknowledge that. I particularly liked the homophony of 'hear' and 'here', and the initial half-line's resistance to a separate, extra-metrical translation of *Hwæt* (which Heaney so brilliantly translated as 'So'.)

The revisions, the new work lasted through January and February 2016. Chemotherapy was into its fourth month, with two more months to come. A note at the end of the draft typescript tells me that the translation – something begun so partially and uncertainly in 2005 – was completed in draft on 22 February 2016. But translations, like the poems with which they're in dialogue, are never really finished. They are only put by, and there was much still to do even if the dragon had been dumped unceremoniously off a cliff.

There will I imagine be those who will think that the foregoing has been special pleading. Not at all: in life, work and illness alike there's little alternative to remaining as matter-of-fact as possible, and working on the *Beowulf* translation during chemo helped me to stay matter-of-fact and kept me away from the alternatives (the antiques and the vegetables). Yet it did one further thing: it exposed a debt I ought here to acknowledge. Many years earlier, before his untimely death, my old friend and colleague Steve Glosecki (then of the University of Alabama at Birmingham) had worked on his own translation of *Beowulf*, and many were the emails we'd exchanged about his engagement with the poem. Steve worked almost to the end, and we corresponded almost to the end. He always referred to the cancer that would kill him as 'the dragon' or 'the beast' – and tragically, unimaginably, in Steve's final battle it was the dragon who won.

Steve Glosecki was a hero, the kindest of men. His heroism, gentleness and insight set me an example, and Steve was very present to me as I worked again on Beowulf's mortal encounter with the legendary beast. In truth I doubt I'd ever have finished the present draft translation had it not been for Steve's courage and his prior example. In many ways, we finished *Beowulf* together. Had I not other and even more pressing debts to pay, this work, imperfect though it is, would have been dedicated to him.

*

What version of the line and half-line was I using in the present translation? Essentially, and mindful of Tolkien's aside (quoted above) that this kind of verse seemed 'more like masonry than music', I was using a four-position half-line with very strong closural constraints. The four position half-line I had learned from Tom Cable (1991) and the closural constraints from one of the first of my great teachers, Barbara Strang (1970). Elsewhere I had briefly and partially explored what these constraints were and how, theoretically, they might work in a textbook chapter of my own (McCully and Hilles 2005, chapter 5), but in the present translation the task was less theoretical: it was to get these constraints to work as verse so that the poem proceeded to impart information piece by piece, half-line by half-line, while not overlooking those patterns of thematic interlace found so often in the original.

POSITION

What do I mean by 'position'? A position is an abstract and underlying element of the metrical composition that is obligatorily filled with linguistic material – with one or more syllables. A half-line spanning exactly four syllables will, accordingly, match exactly with the positions that underlie it:

wuldres Waldend   188a
 1   2   3 4

strēamas wundon   212b
 1 2   3   4

Yet there are many half-lines containing more than four syllables. In these instances, a position may be filled with one or more unstressed syllables, but these syllables must be of a particular morphological composition, i.e. they must be 'function words' – prepositions, articles, relativisers, pronouns, some adverbs, high-frequency non-lexical verbs (such as *have* and *be*) and so on:

bāt under beorge   211a – position 2 expanded to span *under*
1 2   3 4

Nō hēr cūðlīcor   244a – position 1 expanded to span *Nō hēr*
1   2 3 4

One of the most important findings of Cable (1991), however, is that only one position may be expanded in any given half-line. That is, unstressed syllables don't occur unconstrained – which in turn provides a problem for those favouring quasi-musical readings of the poem's metre or even those believing that *Beowulf* is composed in a 'strong stress' metre in which unstressed syllables occur with abandon. They do not. Cable's observation on exactly how they are constrained shows up particularly in those half-lines that earlier scholarship, following the great work of Sievers in the nineteenth century (1885), dubbed B-type half-lines, i.e. those falling into a 'rising' pattern: x / x /. Notionally, both unstressed positions could be expanded (thus x x / x x / or x x x / x x /) – but this doesn't happen: if position 1 is here expanded, position 3 is not, and vice versa.

Throughout the present translation I have tried to observe this constraint on position (and expanded positions) as accurately as possible:

> while he lives at home   21b – position 1 expanded
>   1   2   3   4

> They bore him at the end   28a – position 3 expanded
>   1   2   3   4

The constraint on position also maps into a compositional fix. In line 28b, for instance, 'to brink of the tide', I could have translated normatively as 'to the brink of the tide', but this would have been to allow two positions in the putative half-line to be expanded and thereby, incidentally, to allow an unwanted triple rhythm (de-de-DUM de-de-DUM) to seep into the translation. The first article, therefore – to *the* brink – seemed vulnerable, though I suppose I might equally have translated as *to the brink of tide*. The final result was a half-line that had been stripped of one of its articles. Rightly or wrongly, this kind of procedure I undertook throughout.

In the original as in the translation, no half-line has fewer than four syllables (= four positions).

CLOSURE

One might ask why it is – over the six thousand and more half-lines of *Beowulf*, as indeed across almost all the Old English verse canon – that position 4 in any half-line is never expanded (that is, half-lines never end DUM-de-de). The answer lies in Strang's observation that '[t]here is between half-lines a break, or line-end marker [...] The end of a half-line is always determinate [...] [I]f it is occupied by a lift [stressed syllable: McC] that goes without saying, but if it is occupied by a drop <u>there is the special restriction that the drop must there be monosyllabic</u>' (1970, p.326, my emphasis).

Like the position constraint, the closure constraint is specifically *metrical. Beowulf* is not composed in a 'loosely alliterative rhythm' that allows for 'gabbles of weaker syllables', but is highly wrought and finished. In the half-lines from the original cited above, for example, position 4 is either some kind of stressed (mono)syllable or spans exactly one unstressed syllable:

| wuldres Waldend | 188a – position 4 = one unstressed syllable |
| 1   2   3   4 | |

| strēamas wundon | 212b – position 4 = one unstressed syllable |
| 1   2   3   4 | |

And in the following half-lines, position 4 spans some kind of stressed syllable:

| Flota stille bād | 301b – position 4 = stressed monosyllable |
| 1 2   3   4 | |

| wlanc Wedera lēod | 341a – position 4 = stressed monosyllable |
| 1   2   3 4 | |

This closure constraint, too, I tried to observe as accurately as possible:

while he lives at home   21b – position 4 = stressed monosyllable
1   2   3   4

They bore him at the end   28a – position 4 = stressed monosyllable
1   2   3   4

too long lordless   14b – position 4 = one unstressed syllable
1   2   3   4

COMPOUNDING, SECONDARY STRESS AND ADJACENCY

Most students of *Beowulf* and other Old English verse know that Anglo-Saxon poets make a liberally creative use of compound words. If I open a page of *Beowulf* at random I come across compounds such as *ferhð-frecan* ('eager-hearted (ones)'), *sweord-bealo* ('sword-bale'), *sǣ-sīðe* ('sea-journey'). Such high frequency doesn't necessarily mean, of course, that compounding was a process unique to poetry, though some compounds ('in geār-da-gum') seem antique, time-hallowed and may well have begun life as verse-specific. Yet in Old English as in present-day English, compounding is one the more (if not the most) productive ways of generating new words: *bus-stop, paper-weight, computer-table, light-bulb, lamp-shade...*

Compounds are valuable to Anglo-Saxon poets because (i) they are thematically economical and (ii) because they often provide a good fit with the metrical requirements of the half-line.

First, and in terms of economy, it's useful for the poet to be able to refer to the Christian God as *Līf-frēa* ('Life-lord', line 16b) because *frēa* is also a term used of a secular chieftain, and thus the compound itself limns both Christian and secular worlds. Similarly, it's economical to refer to the highly significant process of generosity via the compound *feoh-giftum* ('fee-gifts', line 21b), where *feoh* spans a range of meanings including 'property, money, wealth' (in the Wrenn/Bolton Glossary). It's telling, too, that the first glimpse we have of the inhabitants of the Danish court is summed up in the compound *driht-guman*, literally 'lord's (Hrothgar's)-men'... or is that, given the context, 'Lord's (God's)-men'?

Second, because compounds – even inflected compounds – so often span two, three, more rarely four syllables they are hugely useful words to match with the four positions required of the half-line:

heal-ærna mǣst   77a
  1   2 3   4

hēah ond horn-gēap   82a
  1   2   3   4

In 82a, however, there's another thing to notice with respect to the usefulness of these compound patterns. Linguistically, the second element of the compound *horn-gēap* (glossed as 'wide gabled' in Wrenn) bears secondary stress; metrically, however, the final syllable counts in the pattern like any other lesser- or unstressed syllable because it *doesn't stand adjacent to any lesser stressed syllable in the same half-line*. Compare 77a and 82a again: in the first example, the first syllable of *ærna* bears secondary stress (it is the second syllable of the compound *heal-ærn*, 'hall-building', and is adjacent to an unstressed inflection *(-a*, genitive pl.). We can't read *ærna* as comprising two weak (unstressed) syllables, because to do so would violate constraints on position:

*heal-ærna mǣst   77a (where * symbolises impermissible)
  1 2   3

And so the former reading (four positions) makes more sense because it is built of the interplay between linguistic stress and purely metrical demands. In the second example, *horn-gēap* bears a linguistic secondary stress (like e.g. *–fly* in *fire-fly* or *–bulb* in *light-bulb*) yet not a metrical one: all that counts, metrically, is that *gēap* is a monosyllable that is less stressed than the first element of the compound of which it's a part. Elsewhere (McCully and Hilles 2005, chapter 5) I called this patterning a metrical constraint on adjacency.

Effectively, this means that compounds can be plugged into the half-line in the first two or three positions:

poet's	clear-voiced	song		90a
1	2	3	4	

battle-hardened	men			172b
1	2	3	4	

or, using two compounds, across an entire half-line

fine-wrought	war-things			38a
1	2	3	4	

or can stand in the final two positions of the half-line when the second element of the compound is a monosyllable:

across	dark	whale-roads		10a
1	2	3	4	

rucking	under	cliff-falls		211a
1	2	3	4	

Constraints on the form and use of compound words, then, I tried to observe throughout with as much accuracy as my understanding would permit.

RESOLUTION

In the opening section of this *Afterword* I referred to the phenomenon known as 'resolution', whereby two syllables, the first of
which is short and stressed, may count metrically not as two positions but as one:

ellen fremedon   3b (resolution on freme-)
1 2   3   4

In Old English as in present-day English, syllabification is onset-
maximal, so that the /m/ of *fremedon* is syllabified as the onset of
the second syllable rather than the coda of the first:

fre.me.don (where '.' symbolises the syllable division)

Syllable onsets don't count towards calculations of length, so that
in assessing the length or otherwise of the first two syllables of *fre.
me.don* one looks at the 'e' of the first syllable (one vowel segment
= short) and the 'e' of the second (one vowel segment = short). Similar examples can be found in e.g.:

on fæder bearme   21b
1   2   3   4

(resolution on *fæder* – fæ.der)

monegum mǣgþum   5a
  1   2   3   4

(resolution on first two syllables of *monegum* – mo.ne.gum)

I also noted above, following a long and distinguished line of
scholars who have described the phenomenon, that under certain

circumstances resolution could be suspended, namely (and as Tera-sawa – cited above – claims):

a) where the potentially resolvable sequence is preceded by a stressed and long syllable in the same metrical constituent
b) where the resolvable sequence has a minimally bimoraic second syllable

In the present translation I tried to reproduce some of the textures I found in the original by allowing optional resolution of short, stressed syllables and also tried to observe suspension of resolution under condition (a), though I adapted that condition so that resolution could in this translation be suspended if the potentially resolvable sequence was preceded by *any* long or heavy syllable, including those found in function words. It was, I confess, too difficult for me to suspend resolution under condition (b) above as well: a later translator might want to try to adopt that condition and do better than I. The result of my compromise were half-lines such as the following:

how sped by courage	2b (resolution on courage)
1 2 3 4	

(NB. What counts is of course the *phonological* not the *graphic* form of the word in question: *courage* may be spelt with two written vowel shapes in its first syllable – <ou> – but phonemically it has a short vowel there: /kʌɹɪdʒ/.)

honour helped him flourish	11a (resolution on honour and flourish)
1 2 3 4	

Scyld's after-comer	18a (resolution on –comer)
1 2 3 4	

Always it's fitting   19a (resolution on fitting)
1   2   3 4

(syllabification: /fɪ.tɪ.../; *it's* is segmentally heavy – short vowel followed by two consonants)

their ring-giver   35a (suspended resolution on –giver)
   1   2   3 4

(syllabification: /gɪ.və/; *ring-* is stressed and segmentally heavy – short vowel followed by consonant)

FUDGES AND WORRIES

It was this partial set of metrical constraints – closure, position, compounding and adjacency, resolution – that formed some of the equipment I took to the task of translating *Beowulf*. This equipment, however, even while it allowed me to construct half-lines that were a pastiche (a term to which I'll return) of the textures and structures of their originals, wasn't flexible enough to allow me to create a truly metrical translation. Nor, as it turned out, was I absolutely faithful even to the modest set of constraints I'd adopted.

One of the problems I confronted but failed to solve was alignment. In the original, half-lines are usually phrasal units: their metrical closures are also syntactic ones, so there's a coincidence, at the right edge of each half-line, between metrical and phrasal constituents. Consider as a typical specimen the following four lines (28–31), where ']' marks the right edge of a syntactic constituent:

Hī hyne þā ætbǣron]   tō brimes faroðe],
They him then bore away]   to of-sea the current]

swǣse gesīþas],   swā hē selfa bǣd],
dear retainers/companions],   as he himself had asked],

þenden wordum wēold]	wine Scyldinga],
while with-words he wielded]	leader of-Scyldings],
lēof land-fruma]	lange āhte].
beloved land-leader]	(who had) long reigned].

'His dear companions bore him away to the sea currents, just as he himself had asked while he, long-reigning leader of Scyldings and their beloved king, still ruled words.'

In the present translation:

They bore him at the end   to brink of the tide,
his chosen men,   as their chief had asked
when he wielded words   like weapons; carried him   30
and his reputation   to the tide's slow brim.

Overlooking the semantic problem posed by the verb *āhte* (from *āgan*, to own or possess, and therefore requiring some sort of syntactic object), the original is highly appositional: Scyld is revealed both as a leader (or 'friend') – *wine* – and as beloved – *lēof*. The fact that he was such a powerful and durable king is emphasised, and his reputation – as a chieftain 'who overturned the mead-tables of many other tribes' – has already been established by the poet. Therefore it seemed legitimate to me as a translator to try to capture those aspects of great Scyld's life and character even at the moment when his corpse is being prepared for its final sea-journey. Yet I couldn't do this without allowing one cardinal (and determinedly non-literal) structure to span over a half line: *when he wielded words / like weapons*. Other syntactic breaks in the translation here are less obtrusive: *asked* is followed by a syntactic break (the verb is post-modified by the adverbial clause 'when he wielded words'); *carried him* is followed by a co-ordinated phrase ('him / and his reputation'); and *reputation* is followed by a prepositional phrase whose function is adverbial.

The point I'm making is that although I could be faithful to some of the demands of right-alignment I found in the original, semantic and thematic demands also meant that in many places I couldn't deploy every half-line tidily, and phrases spilled over their metrical bounds. As I revised, however, I tried to work in such a way as to strip both earlier drafts and the present translation of obtrusive and wilful bits of overspill:

> Always it's fitting   that a fine young man
> ensure allegiance   in his later years   20
> by giving liberally   while living at home,
> still under his father's   first protection,
> so that in future troubles   his retainers **will be bound**
> **mutually, by loyalty:**   all men prosper
> when **gold-gifts are   good** and great their giver.   25

(abandoned draft; overspillings boldened; further problems here relate to diction: while *bound/mutually* isn't an impossible structure, *mutually/loyally/liberally* all occur here, each with their suffix *-ly*, and that to me read clumsi... ly)

> Always it's fitting   that a fine young man
> secure loyalty   for his later years   20
> by lavish gift-giving   while he lives at home,
> still under his father's   first sheltering,
> so that whatever maulings come,   his men will be bound
> in memory of promise: all parties thrive
> by unforced gold-gifts,   free-handed givers.   25
> (the present translation)

A second problem was posed by extrametricality. As Russom (1987, 1998) has so astutely revealed, certain morphemes may not everywhere count in the metrical pattern. Among these morphemes are the prefix *ge-*, the negative particle *ne* and the conjunction *gē-* (in constructions such as *gē... gē*, 'both... and...'). In the original there's a degree of optionality about this: in a half-line such as *sibbe ne wolde* (154b – 'he didn't intend peace'), position 2 is occupied by the unstressed syllables *–be ne* and it's irrelevant whether this position is filled by one or two unstressed syllables: *sibbe wolde* would notionally be a perfectly well-formed pattern. A half-line such as *gē wið fēond gē wið frēond* (1864a – 'both against enemy and against friend') looks at first glance to be metrically deviant because positions 1 and 3 are both expanded... until one strips away extrametrical *gē-*. Somewhat similarly, in the present translation I've allowed negative particles (*not, n't*) and conjunctions (*and, but, or*) sometimes to count in the metrical pattern and sometimes not. In the following, for instance, the half-lines would be metrical if one stripped away all instances of 'or' (translating the original's *oððe*):

'[...] but presently it shall be
'that sickness or the sword   shall unseat your strength,
'or the flames' embrace,   or the flood's whelming,
'or the blade in spite,   or the spear in flight,   1765
'or the horror of age,   or the once-keen eyes
'failing, dim-shadowed;   and soon it shall be due
'to you, dear warrior: death shall overpower you.'

A third problem was posed by suffixes. In the present translation I have allowed half-lines such as *most blessedly* (100a). To be sure, this has four syllables matching the four positions of the underlying pattern, but such a half-line ends on two unstressed syllables, thus breaking one prime constraint on half-line construction, namely that half-line-final drops must be monosyllabic; a similar deviant half-line occurs in *winning integrity* (349a). Under the constraints by which I was trying to work, both half-lines (and there are others of similar composition) are deviant. Some metrical theories, however, and notably that of Russom, allow half-lines to end on two unstressed syllables provided those syllables are part of the same word. Thus Russom reads 144a, *Swā rīxode* ('So he ruled') as ending on two unstressed syllables spanning the verb suffix *-ode*. Technically I think there's a case for reading *-od –* here (and elsewhere) as syllabically heavy, at least diachronically (the suffix derives from earlier *-ōd(e)*), and this in turn may point up the supposition that Old English metre was inherently archaising. Yet the supposition didn't help my case as a translator: either I could occasionally allow half-lines that were by my own constraints metrically deviant (while smiling gratefully at Russom and others), or I could redraft, or paraphrase, or find some other way around the problem. I tried all three remedies, and none of them worked particularly well. Accordingly, I left the metrically deviant half-lines in the present translation.

A fourth problem – I'll here call it a fourth and final problem, though there were many others with which I wrestled – was posed by alliteration. Everyone knows that (i) alliteration is a property of stressed syllables and (ii) that generally speaking *two syllables* in the first half-line alliterate, and in turn alliterate with *one* syllable in the second half-line (so-called aa: ax alliteration):

Hī hyne þā ætbǣron]	tō brimes faroðe],
	see below
They him then bore away]	to of-sea the current]
swǣse gesīþas],	swā hē selfa bæd],
/s/ /s/	/s/ alliteration /s/
dear retainers/companions],	as he himself had asked],
þenden wordum wēold]	wine Scyldinga],
/w/ /w/	/w/ alliteration /w/
while with-words he wielded]	leader of-Scyldings],

lēof land-fruma]	lange āhte].
/l/ /l/	/l/ alliteration /l/
beloved land-leader]	(who had) long reigned].

There's at least one variant pattern in the original. It's occasionally the case that the first half-line contains only one alliterating syllable, but if so, this syllable occurs in the first, the only or the most-stressed lexical word of that half-line:

Hī hyne þā ætbǣron]	tō brimes faroðe],
/b/	/b/ alliteration /b/
They him then bore away]	to of-sea the current]

on flōdes ǣht	feor gewītan
/f/	/f/ alliteration /f/
in of-flood power]	far go]

In another original variant, finite verbs – particularly high-frequency verbs – occurring early in the clause and the half-line alliterate optionally:

hēah ofer hēafod,	lēton holm beran	
/h/ /h/	/h/	alliteration /h/
high over head],	let sea to-bear (him)]	

(*lēton* is finite verb but occurs early in the clause and half-line = doesn't alliterate).

All this is well-known – for an excellent summary see Terasawa 2011, pp.3–7. In terms of translation, I suppose theoretically it would just about be possible to follow the alliterative constraints of the original. Occasionally, I have even done so, usually through one of the variant alliterative patterns available:

'It's no deep secret,   dear lord Hygelac: 2000
   /d/   /d/
'many a man knows now   of the mighty fight,
    /m/   /m/

'the great contest,   between Grendel and me...
  /g/   /g/

And sporadically I was able to deploy standard alliteration:

'it's rare for the spear   to rest anywhere,   2030
'to blunt or bend,   whatever the bride's value.'
 /b/   /b/   /b/

Yet more often, it proved impossible to deploy standard alliterative patterns line after line. For one thing, to do so would have obliged me to have inverted standard word order, or to use or invent words obscure and inaccurate; for another, the aural result seemed to me less than satisfactory: the alliteration became too intrusive. If I'm right about such intrusiveness, I wonder why it should be that contemporary ears perceive an alliterative pattern as intrusive when ears of twelve hundred years ago would have found a similar pattern both significant and even praiseworthy?

And so I fudged. For once, I'm not alone: in their very different but equally splendid translations, both Morgan (2002) and Heaney (1999) used a version of the long line in which alliteration, if present at all (almost invariably in Heaney, less often in Morgan), falls indifferently on stressed syllables in first and/or second half-lines:

Will **feast unfearing** in the warriors' hall
(Morgan, line 443; alliteration first half-line only)

And **work of Wayland. Fate must be fate!**
(Morgan, line 455; alliteration internal to each half-line)

In the joy of the pride of life. An attendant
(Morgan, line 494; no alliteration)

'How did you **fare** on your **foreign** voyage,
(Heaney, line 1987; alliteration on last stressed syllable of first half-line, first stressed syllable of second)

Dear **Beowulf,** when you **abruptly** decided
(Heaney, line 1988; alliteration on last stressed syllable of first half-line, first stressed syllable of second)

To **sail** away across the **salt** water...'
(Heaney, line 1989; alliteration on first stressed syllable of first half-line, first stressed syllable of the second)

'On the **Danes** glitter   **dear-bought** heirlooms,   2035
'**hardened**, ring-locked –   **Heathobard** treasures,
'worn in **battle**   as long as **battle** lasted,
'until they'd **witnessed**   **warriors'** destruction,
'the **lives** of friends   **lost** in shield-shatter,
'**beloved** companions   **led** into slaughter.   2040
(this translation)

The result was imperfect, but it was the best I could do without further mashing and mangling. I also followed the lead of the original in allowing /sk/, /sp/ and /st/ to alliterate only with, respectively, /sk/, /sp/ and /st/, though very rarely (and this would have been debarred by any *scop*) I allowed such clusters to alliterate with /s/:

stiffened with anger   I **stood** upright   2092

steep place of **stones**.   His **sty's** entrance   2213

spell-burnished rims,   at the building's **spur**   326

best of **strongholds,** was **beset,** unused 412
(alliteration of /st/ – strongholds – with /s/ – beset)

I hope I've said enough here to indicate something of how I went about my business as a translator. The constraints were many, the successes few. Disconcertingly, too, I kept remembering a slighting comment by one twentieth-century critic (in a reference I still haven't been able to track down and revisit) to the effect that expending ingenuity and energy in creating a metrical translation of such ancient materials was finally to have created a *pis aller* – a stopgap, or possibly, a last resort of the desperate. And after all (I started to asked myself), was it worth it?

WHY?

I've already indicated two reasons why I undertook this work: one was to correct an earlier false start; the other was to honour a personal debt. A third reason – again alluded to in the foregoing – was my increasing professional interest in the epic genre. Yet there were other reasons too.

I imagine that some readers will think that in undertaking this translation I am in some way measuring myself against some very august forebears. There are after all some wonderful translations, just as I had access to grammars, dictionaries, even word-for-word transliterations. Of those last I found the literal gloss on www. heorot.dk particularly helpful when it came to disambiguating and understanding some of the knottier passages, especially those found towards the end of the poem. Even using a gloss, however, there were still the tasks of translation within the constraints my understanding of the poem had set for itself. In the previous section I detailed some (though not all) of those tasks.

It may be found strange that I relatively rarely looked at others' translations when I was actively translating myself. There were instances where I did – looking up, for example, how others had translated dual pronouns, or cross-checking smaller narrative incidents. Yet generally I preferred to work in my own way, by which I mean again 'within the constraints I'd set for myself'. Nor, perhaps wickedly, did I consult any works on translation theory. To engage with translation theory would have diverted me into old intellectual alignments (that is, I would engage while wearing a long-abandoned philologist's helmet) and even worse, would have taken time away from what I then saw as a primary activity – actually wrestling with the new translation. The fact that I scarcely referenced other translations until my own work was finished is less defensible. Any such defence would rest on the fact that like most writers I'm a fairly good mimic. Heaney's 1999 translation, for example, is so strong, and so characteristic of his own gifts as a poet, that to read Heaney's translation at the same time as I was attempting to create my own would have been merely to construct a re-working of Heaney. And I wanted to create more than a re-working of another contemporary translation. (Nevertheless, the reader will find in the present work one very clear reference to Heaney, in line 1652, where I allow Beowulf to open an address to Hrothgar with the single word 'So' – which was a profound gesture of acknowledgement from one translator to his great predecessor.) To create more than a re-working of Heaney, or Morgan, or Tolkien (2014) or Liuzza (1999) meant engaging in the first instance not with others' translations but with those constraints inherent in (or inferred to inhere in) the original poem. Even those translations whose principles seemed closest to my own – I think in the first instance of Liuzza's wonderful preservation of some of the rhythmicity and alliteration of the original – I avoided. It may sound fanciful, but I suppose in some ways the avoidance was itself an attempt to imagine that I was – no, not a poet, but a scribe or copyist in an Anglo-Saxon scriptorium, someone working in a lambent, candle-lit darkness, trying to puzzle out the constraints on the medium with which he was busy... Or, as I'd put it many years before:

Bede's Copyist

I have no proper name, yet his is tall
On Europe's stones and in the candleflukes
Whose culture briefly held a sparrow's brawl
In a crowned head. We set it down in books,
A lettered Latin – that bird, this birth, that stall –
    With no mistakes.

Outside, the snow almost obscures the park,
Our wooden Christ's obliterated face.
Inside, with all the negligence of grace
His habit falls across my page's mark.
Again we work between space and space –
    And both are dark.
    (from *Time Signatures*, 1993)

Equally, like any scribe, I found that the works most useful were glossaries, dictionaries and footnotes rather than translations whose very brilliance and creativity might well have baffled, chastened or even overwhelmed me.

If, therefore, I lacked the ambition to measure myself against some very great forebears, why did I do what I did?

It was at least partly a matter of trying to expose what I believed (and still believe) are some essential continuities between the English language of twelve hundred years ago and the English language of the present day. If I'd thought that the language and metre of *Beowulf* was so remote from us as to exist in quite another Germanic tongue, one only to be visited while in possession of a grammar and a dictionary, I would probably have left the poem to its scholarly specialists and its story to an antiquarian twilight. Yet – and for all that I once worked, fairly intensively, on matters relating to historical linguistics and language change – the more I translated, the more I found myself entering a set of *continuities*, and continuities sustained, moreover, by a constituency of voices. Here, too, a passage from another very fine contemporary writer supported and encouraged me:

> What strikes me about English – and other languages so far as I know them – is constancy rather than change. The language adds to itself, varies and shifts within itself, even contradicts itself, but it has a central nature which, if it changes, changes extremely slowly [...] The language that is current is archaic too; a vast anonymity that we reach back into as soon as we speak. If we are aware of its ancientness we'll have a better sense of its precision as well. [Robert Wells, 1994, p.175 – the essay is, tellingly, called 'Distinctive anonymity']

These continuities seem to operate both on the larger scale – in the fact that epic as a genre has existed since *Gilgamesh* and been re-invented across languages – and on a smaller. To take but one example of this smaller scale: earlier I said something about how secondary stress, compounding and adjacency were deployed in the original Old English materials. I also noted how alliteration works across the two half-lines that make up the long line of Anglo-Saxon verse. Yet textbook materials on 'how alliteration works' often beg a question: why is it, across many thousands of lines of verse whose creation and reception spanned many centuries, does the final stressed syllable of the second half-line rarely if ever alliterate?

The answer was exposed by the formidable scholarship of Russom (1987). Half-lines of Old English verse, he suggested, are themselves constructed like large compound words, with their most prominent elements (comprised of lexical words) lying at their left edges. The line itself is again constructed like a large compound, with its leftmost element (the first half-line) bearing more underlying prominence than its rightmost. Underlyingly, therefore, lines and half-lines pattern as follows, where 'S' symbolises 'more strongly prominent' and 'W' symbolises 'more weakly prominent':

Line of Old English alliterative verse

It appears that weak constituents of weak constituents can't alliterate; further, alliteration preferentially is found in strong (sub-) constituents. I'm not suggesting – nor, I think, would Russom ever suggest – that the lines and half-lines of Old English verse are invariably *pronounced* with strongest stress at their leftmost edges. But I do suggest that this particular patterning is an underlying constraint whose form is rooted in something that occurred in the tenth century just as it does in the twenty-first – namely, compounding. Lines and half-lines are therefore, and in this sense, stylisations of something already happening in the language.

If this is correct then it means that thematically, half-lines are front-loaded: strongest (relative, underlying) prominence falls at their left edges, and it's at this uniquely sensitive place within the half-line that the poet may choose to introduce new, interesting or thematically complex material, allowing a following half-line to provide an appositional comment on that material:

Hrōðgār maþelode,	helm Scyldinga	456
[subject verb],	[appositional comment on subject]	
Hrothgar spoke,	helm/protector of the Scyldings...	

'Secge ic þē tō sōþe,	sunu Ecglāfes,
[subject + verb phrase]	[appositional to 'thee']
I tell you truly,	son of Ecglaf,

'þæt næfre Grendel swā fela	gryre gefremede,

[relative clause, subject Grendel]   [object: horror]
that Grendel would never so much   horror have brought about,

'atol æglæca   ealdre þīnum [...]'   590-92
[appositional to 'Grendel']   [post-modifies 'brought about']
(that) terrible monster   (among) your people [...]

It's this appositional tendency, whose root lies in the poetic potential of compounding and relative prominence, that I tried to
capture:

'I say truly,   son of Ecglaf,   590
'that Grendel would never   have visited such grim,
'humiliating crimes   on Heorot's majesty
'if your doom and courage   had been as dauntless,
'fierce, as durable   as you dare to claim.
'And yet he's discovered   he doesn't have to care! –   595
'hasn't learnt to dread   lashing sword-tumult
'from those vicious victims,   those "victors" the Danes!
'He extracts his toll,   treats all your folk
'to no mercy,   mangles where he pleases,
'slays, sends to death,   receiving no return   600
'from Danish spears [...]'

And this in turn links with the diction I used in the present translation. Occasionally I tried to follow the *Beowulf*-poet in his precise use of compounding, as here, where I've translated original
gūþ-geweorca (literally 'deeds of battle') as follows:

'Nō ic mē an here-wæsmun   hnāgran talige
'gūþ-geweorca   þonne Grendel hine [...]'   677-78

'I count myself nowise inferior in warlike vigour for deeds of battle
than Grendel counts himself' (Wrenn/Bolton 1973, p.123, footnote)

'I count myself no less   keen for battle,
'grim, blood-lustful,   than Grendel himself [...]' (this translation)

Grim and *Grendel* are thematically and alliteratively linked;
blood-lustful (developing the key compound *here-wæsm*) emphasises the physicality of the impending fight, pointed in the following lines, where Beowulf eschews the use of a sword. Throughout,
as I trimmed and adopted, adapted and tailored, I tried to find
a diction that was contemporary and readable yet still relatively
formal. The archaisms that, many years before, I'd found in some
earlier translations – the *Lo!*s and *hither*s, the *olden story*s and the
*welkin*s – I forbade myself to use, though with some compounds
('sword-tumult') I tried to stay flexible and creative. This last was
sometimes to court trouble. Likewise I tried to avoid inversions
of standard word-order, though sometimes adaptations of original
word-order allowed for interesting effects of ambiguity – as here,
where 'cursed, shunned by God' could apply both to Grendel and
the moorland and mist-slopes from which he emerges:

Out of the moorland,   falls of mist-slopes,   710
cursed, shunned by God,   Grendel came walking.
This ravager meant   to harm menfolk,
entrap them by trickery   in the towering hall.
This cloud-walker   came to the building,
and plain in his sight   were the plastered walls [...]   715

Again, compounding does some work: 'cloud-walker' partially
translates a fairly unexceptional line of the original, *[w]ōd under
wolcnum* (line 714a – he advanced under the clouds), and again
stands in an appositional relationship to *Grendel... this ravager...
this cloud-walker.*

Wherever possible I preferred non-Romance words over Latinate
ones. Grevel's early criticism of my abandoned earlier draft was
entirely justified, and so, after excising words such as *vanity* and

valiant from my failed opening, I tried to stick to a quiet, unshowy diction. It wasn't possible to be resolutely Germanic throughout, however (this made the translation sound like something from Hardy or Barnes). While I sometimes permitted myself the antique and native word *byrnie* (for mail coat) I also used the word *corselet* (a French loan originally meaning 'body armour'); preference for one or the other term – neither of which was particularly satisfactory – was driven by the needs of alliteration.

Preference for the native over the Romance also caused me to come a cropper in an earlier draft. The final half-line of the poem (line 3182b) is *ond lofgeornost* – a term that occurs at the end of a list of Beowulf's virtues as a man, leader and king. The compound is built out of the words *lof* and *geornost*, where *geornost*, a superlative, may be translated as something like 'most eager, most desirous, most keen'. That leaves the word *lof* – a term and concept that, like the term and concept *dōm*, is so important that Tolkien devotes an appendix to it in his 1936 essay (pp.38–45). Tolkien pointed out that *lof* 'is ultimately and etymologically *value, valuation*, and so *praise*' and is part of 'the noble pagan's desire for the *merited praise* of the noble' (p.39, Tolkien's emphasis). Recent translators, among them Heaney and Morgan, translate as 'fame' – thus Heaney's translation of *ond lofgeornost* as 'and keenest to win fame' and Morgan's 'most vigilant of fame'. In my false start I tried to lay stress on the fact that Beowulf had been *capable of* winning reputation, i.e. he *knew how to* win fame, and so, having rejected the Romance word *capable*, hit on the word 'couth', translating *ond lofgeornost* as 'and couth in fame' – that is, Beowulf knew how to conduct himself in such a way as to deserve fame. *Couth* – which most people can reconstruct from the word *uncouth* – etymologically derives from the Old English verb *cunnan*, 'to know' or 'to know how to'. One commentator objected, however, calling my use of *couth* 'clunky'. I considered his comment so carefully that I exposed the problem to an audience during a reading at the John Rylands Library in Manchester (2011). There was a pause after the reading, after which one lady put up her hand. 'This problem with *couth*, Chris,' she said. 'It's fine in Bolton, you know. We use *couth* all the time.' I was reassured – but only briefly. There was a further problem with *couth* in that I'd lost the superlative suffix (though I suppose I could have translated as 'most couth'). In the present translation I have excised *couth* and have reverted to something less showy but still Germanic: *and keenest in fame*, where *keenest* derives ultimately from Old English *cēne*.

Before I embarked on the correction of my false start and on completing this translation, I half-expected the process to shed some light on philological and critical matters such as the dating of the original. That expectation wasn't fulfilled. It was true that the constraints under which I was working – number of positions per half-line; expanded or unexpanded dips; closure constraints; a partial implementation of Kaluza's Law – made me believe ever more strongly that the poet who composed *Beowulf* was highly literate and his metre largely scriptist. Were the creation of this work to have been modulated by oracy I'd have expected to have encountered more poetic formulae and stock diction. As things stand, and if the constraints were correct, then *Beowulf*'s metre (as I understood it) suggested a later dating rather than an earlier one. Yet here again, metrical criteria for dating were themselves problematic – as Fulk (1992) showed nearly thirty years ago. And therefore I could draw no conclusions about the date of *Beowulf* from what work I completed; I only knew, always and everywhere, that I was dealing with a *poem* written by a supremely skilled poet.

I also looked for prior works of scholarship on the constraint-based model with which I was trying to translate. I found Getty's (2002) work on constraint-based approaches to Old English metre provocative and useful, especially his discussion of the modifications made to Sievers' *typentheorie* by Bliss (1958), but couldn't see the motivation for ascribing prefixes occurring at the left edges of certain half-lines to exceptional, degenerate 'feet' (p.176). Nor did I find in Getty a sufficiently strong statement of the closure constraint that as a translator (and reader) I found so helpful; Getty's 'Boundary (HL)' constraint, for example, simply required that '[b]oundaries between adjacent half-lines should be maximally distinct' (p.243) but this distinctiveness wasn't described in a way I found as concise and convincing as the prior description, given above, in Strang (1970, p.326, cited above). I also berated myself for being thick: by the time I went back to Getty it had been many years since I'd engaged seriously in linguistic metrics, and I found Getty's Optimality-based approach, though hugely promising (my instincts told me), rather difficult to understand. And speaking specifically as an unreliable translator, did I *need* to understand it?

All in all, and sticking to what were a comparatively primitive set of constraints, I most enjoyed translating where I could stick most closely to the original. This cleaving was a preventive against wilfulness and miscalculation. Very occasionally, and usually to fill a half-line, I added a word, possibly a phrase; in one place I translated non-assonantal syllables into a bare handful of line-internal half-rhymes, simply because I was entranced by the pattern and the resulting emphasis; and always, I considered and re-considered. Whether the considering resulted in something worthwhile is for the reader to judge. I merely tried to be consistent within the limits I'd set for myself, and in doing so began to sense further answers to the question as to why I was doing this: it was quietly to rejoin a constituency of voices; to explore continuities; and to learn both tact and humility.

I quite realise now that my earlier belief – that I could somehow construct a fully metrical translation of *Beowulf* in present-day English – was mistaken. What I could and eventually did construct was a pastiche. Now, the word 'pastiche' implies in some literary circles the modifier 'mere'. 'McCully's translation of *Beowulf*? A mere pastiche…'

Around the concept *pastiche* swirl a number of other terms – parody, imitation, 'influence'. It's probable that many younger poets are willy-nilly caught in the grip of pastiche as they contend with (that is, are influenced by) the work of their precursors. Their intentions – perhaps, after all, I am speaking of my own former intentions – are by no means parodic, if by *parody* we understand a partial imitation constructed so as to have a social or political, humorous intent. Nor are those early works of homage specifically imitative; an imitation, to be an imitation, presumably appropriates as much as possible of the structural features of the original. If, therefore, parody is partial, and imitation is more thoroughgoing, where does that leave pastiche?

One could take two radically different views of pastiche. One would be to follow Bloom (1973) and suggest that pastiche characteristically occurs when a younger or belated poet attempts to re-write the work of a 'stronger' precursor, and to do so by wilful misreading (what Bloom calls 'misprision': *The Anxiety of Influence*, p.5). On this view, pastiche is, like parody, a partial re-appropriation, though without a humorous end. Yet if I attempt to apply this view to my own encounters with *Beowulf* I'm left queasy. The account would imply I wrestled heroically with the originating text, emerging from the contest victorious, having in some sense – though what sense? – been melancholically chastened and yet re-made by the encounter. Frankly, I'm unwilling to valorise myself or my work here in those terms.

A second, possibly more sober view would be an adaptation of Jameson (1991). Commenting on the 'stupendous proliferation of social codes today' (p.17), he interestingly contrasts parody and pastiche:

> In this [i.e. the post-modern] situation parody finds itself without a vocation; it has lived, and that strange new thing pastiche slowly comes to take its place. Pastiche is, like parody, the imitation of a peculiar or unique, idiosyncratic style, the wearing of a linguistic mask, speech in a dead language. But it is a neutral practice of such mimicry, without any of parody's satiric impulse, devoid of laughter [...] Pastiche is thus blank parody. [p.17]

Further, Jameson avers that 'the producers of culture have nowhere to turn but to the past' (pp.17–18) and invokes 'voices stored up in the imaginary museum of a now global culture' (p.18).

Yet if, again, I apply that view to my work on *Beowulf* I can't quite bring myself to believe that the encounter was one of vacuous yet unavoidable historicism. Pastiche has its uses, I think, if it identifies structures and exposes limits – the limits of the language, the limits of the poet (or, as here, the translator). Perhaps it is particularly useful if it can show why a more thoroughgoing imitation *wasn't* possible.

It's true that I sometimes felt as if I were *contending* with the *Beowulf* poet, and to that extent, Bloom may be partially right; I also know – though it took far too long to find out – that after all, I was constructing a pastiche, and to that extent, Jameson may also be right. For what it's worth, I also instinctively incline to the idea that 'stronger' poets (and translators) exist. It was so in my own case, where the strong precursors – to borrow Bloomian terminology – were Auden and, to a lesser extent, Hughes; it seems to be so in many others – Eliot and Laforgue, Pound and Browning, Wordsworth and Milton, Milton and Virgil, Chaucer and Boccaccio. In the case of these very great poets, however, so strong are their creative energies and gifts that even in celebrating their precursors they also transcend them: they make it new. In the present case, my gifts and energies were not great enough to make anything new. If I sought anything, I sought a form of creative self-effacement. I could not transcend *Beowulf* and in any case, to generate a transcendental translation of *Beowulf* (I smile as I write) would be to create a new poem. I preferred not to 'make it new' but to 'make the old anew' and if the resulting work is truly a pastiche then it comes from goodwill and at least has avoided the perils of becoming pastiche's grinning twin, a parody. Further, the metrical, narrative and thematic limits of this pastiche were themselves intriguing, and in turn generated further new work in the form of the synoptic epics to which I have referred elsewhere.

There was a final reason why I undertook the present translation. Many years ago (in 1981) my professor and tutor, Barbara Strang, pointed me in the direction of a paper by Marjorie Daunt (1946). In 'Old English verse and English speech rhythm' Daunt suggested that '[i]f an audience is to listen for any length of time to a recited narrative [...] the medium [...] must follow the natural language' and argued that '[m]odern spoken English has preserved much of the pre-Conquest speech rhythm'. She gave examples from speeches, newspapers and political catchphrases to support her view, and concluded that Old English verse is 'a tidied form of the spoken language' (p.66).

I was curious, back then; these days I would still ask how the relevant tidying was done. Yet if I remember the undergraduate I was – anxious, arrogant, too eager to please – with distaste, I also remember the interest (and the subsequent work) my exposure to Daunt's paper generated, and the kindness with which Professor Strang encouraged my interests. I doubt very much that she would have approved of the work that appears here, but her perceptiveness would, I think, have recognised the persistence with which one man, now middle-aged and conscious both of his intellectual limits and his mortality, has endeavoured to join himself up with the better part of a self he once was – or imagined himself to be.

Chris McCully
Essex
2018

SELECTED REFERENCES
&
FURTHER READING

Print

Alexander, Michael (1973) *Beowulf: A Verse Translation*. London: Penguin.

Bjork, Robert E. and John D. Niles (eds, 1997) *A Beowulf Handbook*. Exeter: University of Exeter Press.

Bliss, A.J. (1958) *The Metre of* Beowulf. Oxford: Blackwell.

Bloom, Harold (1973) *The Anxiety of Influence: A Theory of Poetry*. Oxford: Oxford University Press.

Chickering, Howell et al. (eds., 2014) *Teaching* Beowulf *in the Twenty-First Century*. Tempe, Arizona: Arizona Center for Medieval and Renaissance Studies.

Creed, R.P. (1966) 'A new approach to the rhythm of *Beowulf*'. *Publications of the Modern Languages Association* 81, pp. 23–33.

Creed, R.P. (1990) *Reconstructing the Rhythm of* Beowulf. Columbia: University of Missouri Press.

Daunt, Marjorie (1946) 'Old English verse and English speech rhythm.' *Transactions of the Philological Society*, pp. 56–72.

Fulk, R.D. (1992) *A History of Old English Meter*. Philadelphia: Pennsylvania University Press.

Getty, Michael (2002) *The Metre of* Beowulf: *A Constraint-based Approach*. Berlin and New York: Mouton de Gruyter.

Hadbawnik, David and Sean Reynolds (eds., 2011) 'Jack Spicer's *Beowulf*. Parts 1 and 2.' New York: City University of New York Graduate Center.

Heaney, Seamus (1999) *Beowulf*. London: Faber and Faber.

Heusler, Andreas (1891) 'Zur geschichten der altdeutschen Verskunst'. *Germanische Abhandlungen* 8, pp.1–159.

Hume, Kathryn (1975) 'The theme and structure of *Beowulf*'. *Studies in Philology* 72 No. 1, pp.1–27.

Hurley, Michael D. and Michael O'Neill (2012) *Poetic Form: An Introduction*. Cambridge: Cambridge University Press.

Jameson, Fredric (1991) *Postmodernisim, or, The Cultural Logic of Late Capitalism*. London and New York: Verso.

Johnston, Andrew James (2014) 'Postcolonial *Beowulf*'. In eds. Chickering et al., pp. 231–240.

Ker, W.P. (1904) *The Dark Ages*. New York: Charles Scribner's Sons.

Ker, W.P. (2012) *Epic and Romance*. [First edition 1908.] www.forgottenbooks.org

Klaeber, F. (1950) *Beowulf, and the Fight at Finnsburg*. 3rd edition. Lexington, Mass.: D.C. Heath.

Lennard, John (2005) *The Poetry Handbook*. Second edition. Oxford: Oxford University Press.

Lévi-Strauss, Claude (1955) 'The Structural Study of Myth'. [https://www.jstor.org/stable/536768]

Liuzza, Roy (1999) *Beowulf*. Peterborough, Ontario: Broadview Literary Texts.

McCully, Chris (1988) *The phonology of English rhythm and metre, with special reference to Old English*. 2 vols. PhD. thesis. Department of English Language and Literature, University of Manchester, UK.

McCully, Chris (1993) *Time Signatures*. Manchester: Carcanet Press.

McCully, Chris (2008) *Old English Poems and Riddles*. Manchester: Fyfield Books/Carcanet Press.

McCully, Chris (2014) '*Beowulf*: the monsters and the translators.' Talk, Research seminar, Department of Literature, Film and Theatre Studies, University of Essex, UK.

McCully, Chris (2016) 'Beowulf's homecoming.' Talk, Essex Book Festival, UK.

McCully, Chris (2017) 'Notes on translating *Beowulf*'. Research seminar, *Contemporary Poetry in Translation*, University of Essex, UK.

McCully, Chris (2017) 'Dragons in Chelmsford'. Talk, Essex Book Festival, UK.

McCully, Chris and Sharon Hilles (2005) *The Earliest English*. Harlow: Pearson Education Ltd.

Morgan, Edwin (2002) *Beowulf*. [First edition 1952.] Manchester: Carcanet Press.

Obst, Wolfgang (1987) *Der Rhythmus des* Beowulf: *Eine Akzent- und Takttheorie*. Heidelberg: Carl Winter.

Obst, Wolfgang (1996) 'Can Old English rhythm be reconstructed?' In eds. Chris McCully and J.J. Anderson, *English Historical Metrics*. Cambridge: Cambridge University Press, pp. 59–72.

Olson, Charles (1992) *The Maximus Poems*. Ed. George F. Butterick. Berkeley: University of California Press.

Osborn, Marijane (2014) 'Visualizing the material culture of *Beowulf*.' In eds. Chickering et al., pp.185–93.

Papadopoulos, Renos K. (ed., 2002) 'Refugees, home and trauma' in *Therapeutic Care for Refugees. No Place Like Home*. London: Karnac, pp. 9–40.

Pope, Alexander (2015) *The Iliad of Homer*. [Pope's translation, 1715–20. On some background to the making of Pope's translation, see http://rbscp.lib.rochester.edu/3948.] Indiana: Ex Fontibus Co.

Pope, John C. (1966) *The Rhythm of* Beowulf. [Second, revised edition.] New Haven: Yale University Press.

Preminger, Alex et al. (eds., 1974) *Princeton Encyclopedia of Poetry and Poetics*. Enlarged edition. Princeton, NJ: Princeton University Press.

Robertson, Lisa (1997) *Debbie: An Epic*. Vancouver: New Star Books.

Rukeyser, Muriel (2005) 'The Book of the Dead' in *The Collected Poems of Muriel Rukeyser*, eds. Janet E. Kaufman and Anne F.

Herzog. Pittsburgh, PA: University of Pittsburgh Press, p.106ff.

Russom, Geoffrey (1987) *Old English Meter and Linguistic Theory*. Cambridge: Cambridge University Press.

Russom, Geoffrey (1998) Beowulf *and Old Germanic Metre*. Cambridge: Cambridge University Press.

Sievers, Eduard (1885) 'Zur rhythmic des Germanischen alliterationsverses'. *Beiträge zur Geschichte der deitschen Sprache und Literatur* 10, pp. 209–314; 451–545.

Smith, Hazel (2005) *The Writing Experiment: Strategies for Innovative Creative Writing*. Crows Nest: Allen & Unwin.

Stenton, F.M. (1947) *Anglo-Saxon England*. Oxford: The Clarendon Press.

Terasawa, Jun (2011) *Old English Metre: An Introduction*. Toronto: University of Toronto Press.

Tolkien, J.R.R. (1936) 'Beowulf: the Monsters and the Critics'. Sir Israel Gollancz Memorial Lecture, British Academy. London: Proceedings of the British Academy Vol. XXII.

Tolkien, J.R.R. (2014) Beowulf: *A Translation and Commentary*. [London]: Harper Collins.

Walcott, Derek (1990) *Omeros*. London: Faber and Faber.

Wells, Robert (1994) 'Distinctive anonymity'. In ed. C.B. McCully, *The Poet's Voice and Craft*. Manchester: Carcanet, pp. 167–81.

Wrenn, C.L. (ed., revised W.F. Bolton, 1973) *Beowulf, with the Finnesburg Fragment*. London: Harrap.

DVD
Kevin Kiernan (ed., 2011) *Electronic Beowulf*. Third edition. London: British Library

Internet
http://www.heorot.dk/beowulf-rede-text.html
Diacritically marked text and word-for-word gloss, with textual notes. Accessed from 2012 onwards.